FAVORITE BRAND NAME
DESSERTS

D0004988

Publications International, Ltd.

Pictured on the front cover: Fruited Meringue Hearts Melba
(page 324).

Microwave Cooking: Microwave ovens vary in wattage. The
microwave cooking times given in this publication are approximate.
Use the cooking times as guidelines and check for doneness before
adding more time. Consult manufacturer's instructions for suitable
microwave-safe cooking dishes.

FAVORITE BRAND NAME
DESSERTS

Tempting

CAKES & TORTES

Chocolate Cream Torte

1 package DUNCAN HINES® Moist
   Deluxe Devil's Food Cake Mix
1 package (8 ounces) cream cheese,
   softened
½ cup sugar
1 teaspoon vanilla extract
1 cup finely chopped pecans
1 cup whipping cream, chilled
   Strawberry halves, for garnish
   Mint leaves, for garnish (optional)

1. Preheat oven to 350°F. Grease and flour two 8- or 9-inch round cake pans.

2. Prepare, bake and cool cake following package directions for Basic Recipe. Chill layers for ease in splitting.

3. Place cream cheese, sugar and vanilla extract in small bowl. Beat at low speed with electric mixer until smooth. Add pecans; stir until blended. Set aside. Beat whipping cream in small bowl until stiff peaks form. Fold whipped cream into cream cheese mixture.

4. To assemble, split each cake layer in half horizontally. Place one cake layer on serving plate. Spread top with one fourth of filling. Repeat with remaining layers and filling. Garnish with strawberry halves and mint leaves, if desired. Refrigerate until ready to serve.   *Makes 12 to 16 servings*

Deep Dark Chocolate Cake

2 cups sugar
1¾ cups all-purpose flour
¾ cup HERSHEY'S Cocoa or
    HERSHEY'S European Style Cocoa
1½ teaspoons baking powder
1½ teaspoons baking soda
1 teaspoon salt
2 eggs
1 cup milk
½ cup vegetable oil
2 teaspoons vanilla extract
1 cup boiling water
    One-Bowl Buttercream Frosting (recipe
    follows)

Heat oven to 350°F. Grease and flour two 9-inch round
baking pans.* In large bowl, stir together sugar, flour,
cocoa, baking powder, baking soda and salt. Add eggs,
milk, oil and vanilla; beat on medium speed of electric
mixer 2 minutes. Stir in water. (Batter will be thin.)
Pour batter evenly into prepared pans. Bake 30 to 35
minutes or until wooden pick inserted in center comes
out clean. Cool 10 minutes; remove from pans to wire
rack. Cool completely. Prepare One-Bowl Buttercream
Frosting; spread between layers and over top and sides
of cake.   *Makes 8 to 10 servings*

*One 13×9×2-inch baking pan may be substituted for 9-inch round
baking pans. Prepare as directed. Bake 35 to 40 minutes. Cool
completely in pan on wire rack. Frost as desired.

One-Bowl Buttercream Frosting

6 tablespoons butter or margarine, softened
2⅔ cups powdered sugar
½ cup HERSHEY'S Cocoa or HERSHEY'S European Style Cocoa
⅓ cup milk
1 teaspoon vanilla extract

In medium bowl, beat butter until creamy. Add powdered sugar and cocoa alternately with milk, beating well after each addition until smooth and of spreading consistency. Blend in vanilla. Add additional milk, 1 teaspoon at a time, if needed.

Chocolate Chip Layer Cake

1 package DUNCAN HINES® Moist
  Deluxe Yellow Cake Mix
1 package (4-serving size) vanilla instant
  pudding and pie filling mix
4 eggs
1 cup dairy sour cream
½ cup CRISCO® Oil or CRISCO®
  PURITAN® Canola Oil
1 package (6 ounces) semi-sweet
  chocolate chips
1 square (1 ounce) unsweetened
  chocolate, grated
½ cup chopped pecans
2 cups frozen whipped topping, thawed
  and divided
1 container (16 ounces) DUNCAN
  HINES® Creamy Homestyle
  Chocolate Frosting
  Pecan halves, for garnish (optional)

1. Preheat oven to 350°F. Grease and flour three 9-inch round cake pans.

2. For cake, combine cake mix, pudding mix, eggs, sour cream and oil. Beat at medium speed with electric mixer for 2 minutes. Stir in chocolate chips, grated chocolate and chopped pecans. Divide into pans. Bake at 350°F for 35 to 40 minutes or until toothpick inserted in center comes out clean. Cool in pans 15 minutes. Remove from pans; cool completely.

3. To assemble, place one cake layer on serving plate. Spread 1 cup whipped topping over cake. Repeat with remaining layers and whipped topping, leaving top plain. Frost sides and top with Chocolate frosting. Garnish with pecan halves, if desired. Refrigerate until ready to serve. *Makes 12 to 16 servings*

Tip: You can bake this cake in a greased and floured 10-inch Bundt pan or tube pan for 50 to 60 minutes or until toothpick inserted in center comes out clean. Omit whipped topping, Chocolate frosting and pecan halves; dust with confectioners sugar when cooled.

Chocolate Chip Cake

- 2 cups all-purpose flour
- 1 cup packed light brown sugar
- 1 tablespoon baking powder
- 1 teaspoon salt
- ½ teaspoon baking soda
- ½ cup granulated sugar
- ½ cup shortening
- 3 eggs
- 1¼ cups milk
- 1½ teaspoons vanilla extract
- ½ cup semisweet chocolate chips, finely chopped
  Butterscotch Filling (recipe follows)
  Chocolate Chip Glaze (recipe follows)
- ½ cup finely chopped walnuts, divided
  Fresh raspberries (optional)

1. Preheat oven to 350°F. Grease and flour bottom and sides of two 9-inch round baking pans.

2. Combine flour, brown sugar, baking powder, salt and baking soda in small bowl; set aside.

3. Beat granulated sugar and shortening in large bowl with electric mixer at medium speed until light and fluffy, scraping down side of bowl once.

4. Add eggs, 1 at a time, beating well after each addition. Add milk and vanilla; beat at low speed until well blended. Add flour mixture and chocolate chips. Beat at low speed until blended. Beat at medium speed until smooth, scraping bowl occasionally. Pour into prepared pans.

5. Bake 40 to 45 minutes until wooden pick inserted into centers comes out clean. Cool completely on rack.

6. Prepare Butterscotch Filling and Chocolate Chip Glaze. Place 1 cake layer on serving plate. Spread with Butterscotch Filling; sprinkle with ¼ cup walnuts. Top with second cake layer. Pour Chocolate Chip Glaze over top of cake, allowing some of glaze to drip down side of cake. Sprinkle remaining ¼ cup walnuts on top. Garnish with raspberries.   *Makes 8 to 10 servings*

Butterscotch Filling

  ½ **cup packed light brown sugar**
  2 **tablespoons cornstarch**
  ¼ **teaspoon salt**
  ½ **cup water**
  1 **tablespoon butter**

Combine brown sugar, cornstarch and salt in medium saucepan. Add water; cook over medium heat until mixture comes to a boil, stirring constantly. Boil 1 minute, stirring constantly. Add butter; stir until melted. Cool completely.

Chocolate Chip Glaze

  ½ **cup semisweet chocolate chips**
  2 **tablespoons butter**
  1 **tablespoon light corn syrup**

Combine chocolate chips, butter and corn syrup in small saucepan. Cook over low heat until chocolate melts, stirring constantly. Cool slightly.

Chocolate Espresso Cake

2 cups cake flour
1½ teaspoons baking soda
½ teaspoon salt
½ cup margarine or butter, softened
1 cup granulated sugar
1 cup packed light brown sugar
3 eggs
4 squares (1 ounce each) unsweetened chocolate, melted
¾ cup sour cream
1 teaspoon vanilla
1 cup brewed espresso*
Chocolate Frosting (recipe follows)
White Chocolate Curls (recipe follows)

1. Preheat oven to 350°F. Line bottoms of two 9-inch round cake pans with waxed paper; lightly grease paper. Combine flour, baking soda and salt; set aside.

2. Beat margarine and sugars in large bowl with electric mixer at medium speed until light and fluffy. Add eggs, one at a time, beating well after each addition. Add melted chocolate, sour cream and vanilla; beat until blended. Add flour mixture alternately with espresso, beating well after each addition. Pour batter evenly into prepared pans.

3. Bake 35 minutes or until wooden pick inserted into centers comes out clean. Cool layers in pans on wire rack 10 minutes. Loosen edges and invert layers onto rack to cool completely.

4. Prepare Chocolate Frosting. Fill and frost cake with Chocolate Frosting. Place White Chocolate Curls on cake. *Makes 12 servings*

*Use fresh brewed espresso, instant espresso powder prepared according to directions on jar or 1 tablespoon instant coffee powder dissolved in 1 cup hot water.

Chocolate Frosting

- ½ cup margarine or butter, softened
- 4 cups powdered sugar
- 5 to 6 tablespoons brewed espresso, divided
- ½ cup (3 ounces) semisweet chocolate chips, melted
- 1 teaspoon vanilla
  Dash salt

Beat margarine in large bowl with electric mixer at medium speed until creamy. Gradually add powdered sugar and 4 tablespoons espresso; beat until smooth. Beat in melted chocolate, vanilla and salt. Add remaining espresso, 1 tablespoon at a time, until frosting is desired spreading consistency.

White Chocolate Curls

- 2 squares (1 ounce each) white chocolate

Pull a vegetable peeler across both squares of chocolate to create curls. Carefully pick up each chocolate curl by inserting a toothpick into center of the curl. Place on waxed paper-lined baking sheet. Refrigerate 15 minutes or until firm.

HERSHEY'S Special Chocolate Cake

6 tablespoons lower fat margarine (40% oil)
1 cup sugar
1 cup skim milk
1 tablespoon white vinegar
½ teaspoon vanilla extract
1¼ cups all-purpose flour
⅓ cup HERSHEY'S Cocoa
1 teaspoon baking soda
Special Cocoa Frosting (recipe follows)

Heat oven to 350°F. Spray two 8-inch round baking pans with vegetable cooking spray. In medium saucepan over low heat, melt margarine; stir in sugar. Remove from heat. Add milk, vinegar and vanilla; stir until blended. Stir together flour, cocoa and baking soda. Add to sugar mixture; stir with whisk until well blended. Pour batter evenly into prepared pans. Bake 20 minutes or until wooden pick inserted in center comes out clean. Cool 10 minutes; remove from pans to wire racks. Cool completely. Prepare Special Cocoa Frosting. Place one cake layer on serving plate; spread with half the prepared frosting. Place second cake layer

on top; spread remaining frosting over top of cake.
Refrigerate 2 to 3 hours or until chilled. Garnish as
desired. Cover; refrigerate leftover cake.

Makes 12 servings

Special Cocoa Frosting

1 **envelope (1.3 ounces) dry whipped
    topping mix**
1 **tablespoon HERSHEY®S Cocoa**
½ **cup cold skim milk**
½ **teaspoon vanilla extract**

In small, deep mixer bowl with narrow bottom, stir
together topping mix and cocoa. Add ½ cup milk and
½ teaspoon vanilla. Beat on high speed of electric
mixer 4 minutes or until soft peaks form.

Almond Frosting: Omit ½ teaspoon vanilla extract. Add
¼ teaspoon almond extract.

Chocolate Mayonnaise Cake

2 cups all-purpose flour
⅔ cup unsweetened cocoa
1¼ teaspoons baking soda
¼ teaspoon baking powder
3 eggs
1⅔ cups sugar
1 teaspoon vanilla
1 cup HELLMANN'S® or BEST FOODS®
  Real or Light Mayonnaise
1⅓ cups water

1. Preheat oven to 350°F. Grease and flour bottoms of two 9-inch round cake pans.

2. In medium bowl, combine flour, cocoa, baking soda and baking powder; set aside.

3. In large bowl with mixer at high speed, beat eggs, sugar and vanilla, scraping bowl occasionally, 3 minutes or until smooth and creamy. Reduce speed to low; beat in mayonnaise until blended. Add flour mixture in 4 additions alternately with water, beginning and ending with flour mixture. Pour into prepared pans.

4. Bake 30 to 35 minutes or until cake springs back when touched lightly in center. Cool in pans on wire racks 10 minutes. Remove from pans; cool completely on racks. Fill and frost as desired.

Makes one 9-inch layer cake

Cherry Chocolaty Cake

1 **package DUNCAN HINES® Moist Deluxe Dark Chocolate Fudge Cake Mix**
1 **package (8 ounces) cream cheese, softened**
½ **cup butter or margarine, softened**
½ **teaspoon almond extract**
1 **pound confectioners sugar (3½ to 4 cups)**
1 **cup frozen dark sweet cherries, thawed, chopped and well drained**

1. Preheat oven to 350°F. Grease and flour two 9-inch round cake pans.

2. Prepare, bake and cool cake following package directions for Basic Recipe.

3. Combine cream cheese, butter and almond extract in large bowl. Beat at medium speed with electric mixer until smooth. Gradually add confectioners sugar, mixing well after each addition. Measure ¾ cup cream cheese mixture. Place in small bowl; stir in cherries.

4. To assemble, place one cake layer on serving plate. Spread with cherry mixture. Place other layer on top. Frost sides and top with plain cream cheese frosting. Refrigerate until ready to serve.

Makes 12 to 16 servings

Tip: You can use either fresh or canned dark sweet cherries.

Black Forest Cake

**MAZOLA® NO STICK® Corn Oil
  Cooking Spray**
1 **package (18.25 ounces) chocolate cake
  mix plus ingredients as label directs**
Fluffy Frosting (recipe follows)
1 **can (21 ounces) cherry pie filling**
1 **tablespoon cherry flavor liqueur
  (optional)**

1. Preheat oven to 350°F. Spray 2 (9-inch) round cake pans with cooking spray.

2. Prepare and bake cake mix according to package directions for 2 (9-inch) round layers. Cool on wire rack 10 minutes. Remove from pans; cool completely.

3. Place one layer right-side up on cake plate. Spoon a 1-inch-thick ring of Fluffy Frosting around edge of cake.

4. Combine cherry pie filling and liqueur; spoon half onto cake layer, inside frosting ring. Top with second cake layer, bottom-side up.

5. Spread a thin layer of frosting over top of cake. Spread a 2-inch-wide ring of frosting around top edge of cake; generously frost side of cake with remaining frosting. Spoon remaining cherry filling on top of cake, inside frosting.   *Makes 12 servings*

Fluffy Frosting

   2   **egg whites**
   ⅛   **teaspoon salt**
   1   **cup KARO® Light Corn Syrup**
   ¼   **cup sugar**
   1½ **teaspoons vanilla**

1. In large bowl with mixer at high speed, beat egg whites and salt until soft peaks form.

2. In small saucepan combine corn syrup and sugar. Stirring constantly, cook over medium-low heat until sugar dissolves and mixture comes to full boil. Remove from heat.

3. Beating constantly, pour hot syrup into egg whites in a fine steady stream. Beat in vanilla. Continue beating until mixture holds stiff peaks. Use immediately. Makes enough to frost a two-layer 8- or 9-inch cake.   *Makes about 4 cups*

Coconut Cream Cake

CAKE
- 1 package DUNCAN HINES® Moist Deluxe White Cake Mix
- 1 package (4-serving size) coconut cream instant pudding and pie filling mix
- 4 eggs
- 1 cup water
- ⅓ cup CRISCO® Oil or CRISCO® PURITAN® Canola Oil
- ⅓ cup flaked coconut

FROSTING
- 2 cups whipping cream, chilled
- ¼ cup confectioners sugar
- ¼ cup dairy sour cream
- 2½ cups flaked coconut, divided

1. Preheat oven to 350°F. Grease and flour two 9-inch round cake pans.

2. For cake, combine cake mix, pudding mix, eggs, water and oil in large bowl. Beat at low speed with electric mixer until moistened. Beat at medium speed for 2 minutes. Stir in ⅓ cup coconut. Divide evenly into pans. Bake at 350°F for 32 to 37 minutes or until toothpick inserted in center comes out clean. Cool following package directions.

3. For frosting, place whipping cream in another large bowl. Beat at high speed until soft peaks form. Add confectioners sugar and sour cream. Beat until stiff peaks form. Fold in 1½ cups coconut. Fill and frost

cake. Sprinkle with remaining 1 cup coconut.
Refrigerate until ready to serve.

Makes 12 to 16 servings

Tip: Before frosting any cake, let it cool completely.
Never frost a warm cake unless the recipe directs.

Berry Bundt Cake

2 **cups all-purpose flour**
1 **tablespoon baking powder**
1 **teaspoon baking soda**
¼ **teaspoon salt**
1 **cup sugar**
¼ **cup vegetable oil**
¾ **cup buttermilk**
½ **cup cholesterol free egg substitute**
2 **cups frozen unsweetened raspberries**
2 **cups frozen unsweetened blueberries**

1. Preheat oven to 350°F. Spray 6-cup Bundt pan with
nonstick cooking spray. Set aside.

2. Combine flour, baking powder, baking soda and salt
in large bowl. Combine sugar, oil, buttermilk and egg
substitute in medium bowl. Add sugar mixture to flour
mixture; stir just until moistened.

3. Fold in raspberries and blueberries. Pour batter into
prepared pan. Bake 1 hour or until wooden pick
inserted in center comes out clean. Cool in pan on wire
rack. Serve with fresh berries, if desired.

Makes 12 servings

Orange Almond Cake

½   cup vegetable shortening
1   cup honey
1   tablespoon grated orange peel
3   eggs
1¾ cups all-purpose flour
2   teaspoons baking powder
½   teaspoon salt
¼   cup ground blanched almonds
    Honey Whipped Cream (recipe follows)
¼   cup toasted almond slices (optional)
    Orange slices, quartered (optional)

Cream shortening in large bowl with electric mixer.
Gradually add honey, beating until light and fluffy. Add
orange peel. Add eggs, one at a time, beating
thoroughly after each addition. (Mixture may appear
curdled.) Combine flour, baking powder and salt in
small bowl; fold dry ingredients into creamed mixture.
Mix until blended. Add ground almonds; mix well.
Grease bottoms only of two 8-inch round cake pans;
pour in cake batter.

Bake in preheated 325°F oven 30 minutes or until
wooden toothpick inserted in centers comes out clean.
Cool in cake pans on wire racks 10 minutes. Remove

from pans and cool on wire racks. Frost with Honey
Whipped Cream; garnish with toasted almond slices
and orange slices, if desired.

Makes 10 to 12 servings

Honey Whipped Cream

- **1 cup heavy cream**
- **3 tablespoons honey**
- **1 teaspoon vanilla**

Beat cream in medium bowl with electric mixer until
soft peaks form. Gradually add honey; beat until
mixture forms stiff peaks. Fold in vanilla.

Makes about 2 cups

Favorite recipe from **National Honey Board**

Pecan Spice Cake with Browned Butter Frosting

- 1 **package (18 to 19 ounces) moist yellow cake mix**
- ¾ **cup dairy sour cream**
- ¾ **cup water**
- 3 **eggs**
- 1 **tablespoon grated lemon peel**
- 1½ **teaspoons ground cinnamon**
- ½ **teaspoon ground nutmeg**
- ¼ **teaspoon ground allspice**
- 1 **cup chopped pecans**
  Browned Butter Frosting (recipe follows)
  Additional chopped pecans (optional)

1. Preheat oven to 350°F. Grease two 9-inch square baking pans. Combine cake mix, sour cream, water, eggs, lemon peel and spices in large bowl with electric mixer on low speed until ingredients are moistened. Beat on high speed 2 minutes, scraping sides of bowl frequently. Stir in 1 cup pecans. Divide evenly into prepared pans.

2. Bake 25 to 30 minutes until wooden pick inserted in center comes out clean. Cool in pans 10 minutes. Remove from pans to wire racks; cool completely.

3. Place one layer on serving plate. Spread with ⅓ of Browned Butter Frosting. Top with second layer. Frost sides and top of cake with remaining frosting. Garnish with additional pecans, if desired. Store tightly covered at room temperature.　　*Makes 12 to 16 servings*

Browned Butter Frosting

¾　cup butter
5½　cups sifted powdered sugar
1½　teaspoons vanilla extract
　　Dash salt
8　to 9 tablespoons light cream or
　　half-and-half

Heat butter in heavy 1-quart saucepan over medium heat until butter is melted and light amber in color, stirring frequently. Cool butter slightly. Combine browned butter, powdered sugar, vanilla, salt and 8 tablespoons cream in large bowl. Beat on medium speed until smooth and of spreading consistency. Stir in 1 tablespoon cream if frosting is too stiff.

Mom's Favorite White Cake

2¼ cups cake flour
1 tablespoon baking powder
½ teaspoon salt
½ cup margarine or butter, softened
1½ cups sugar
4 egg whites
2 teaspoons vanilla
1 cup milk
Strawberry Frosting (recipe follows)
Fruit Filling (recipe follows)
Fresh strawberries (optional)

1. Preheat oven to 350°F. Line bottoms of two 9-inch round cake pans with waxed paper; lightly grease paper. Combine flour, baking powder and salt in medium bowl; set aside.

2. Beat margarine and sugar in large bowl with electric mixer at medium speed until light and fluffy. Add egg whites, two at a time, beating well after each addition. Add vanilla; beat until blended. With electric mixer at low speed, add flour mixture alternately with milk, beating well after each addition. Pour batter evenly into prepared pans.

3. Bake 25 minutes or until wooden pick inserted into centers comes out clean. Cool layers in pans on wire rack 10 minutes. Loosen edges and invert layers onto rack to cool completely.

4. Prepare Strawberry Frosting and Fruit Filling. To fill
and frost cake, place one layer on cake plate; spread top
with Fruit Filling. Place second layer over filling. Frost
top and sides with Strawberry Frosting. Place
strawberries on top of cake, if desired. Refrigerate;
allow cake to stand at room temperature 15 minutes
before serving.   *Makes 12 servings*

Strawberry Frosting

2 envelopes (1.3 ounces each) whipped
    topping mix
⅔ cup milk
1 cup (6 ounces) white chocolate chips,
    melted
¼ cup strawberry jam

Beat whipped topping mix and milk in medium bowl
with electric mixer on low speed until blended. Beat on
high speed 4 minutes until topping thickens and forms
peaks. With mixer at low speed, beat melted chocolate
into topping. Add jam; beat until blended. Chill
15 minutes or until spreading consistency.

Fruit Filling

1 cup Strawberry Frosting (recipe above)
1 can (8 ounces) crushed pineapple,
    drained
1 cup sliced strawberries

Combine Strawberry Frosting, pineapple and
strawberries in medium bowl; mix well.

Strawberry Shortcake

CAKE
- 1 package DUNCAN HINES® Moist Deluxe French Vanilla Cake Mix
- 3 eggs
- 1¼ cups water
- ½ cup butter or margarine, softened

FILLING AND TOPPING
- 2 cups whipping cream, chilled
- ⅓ cup granulated sugar
- ½ teaspoon vanilla extract
- 1 quart fresh strawberries, rinsed, drained and sliced
- Mint leaves, for garnish

1. Preheat oven to 350°F. Grease two 9-inch round cake pans with butter or margarine. Sprinkle bottom and sides with granulated sugar.

2. For cake, combine cake mix, eggs, water and butter in large bowl. Beat at medium speed with electric mixer for 2 minutes. Pour into pans. Bake at 350°F for 30 to 35 minutes or until toothpick inserted in center comes out clean. Cool in pan 10 minutes. Invert onto cooling rack. Cool completely.

3. For filling and topping, beat whipping cream, sugar and vanilla extract until stiff in large bowl. Reserve ⅓ cup for garnish. Place one cake layer on serving plate. Spread with half the whipped cream and sliced strawberries. Repeat with second layer. Garnish with reserved whipped cream and mint leaves. Refrigerate until ready to serve. *Makes 12 servings*

Strawberry Gingercake

 ½ **cup butter or margarine, softened**
1½ **cups powdered sugar**
 2 **tablespoons ground ginger**
 2 **eggs**
1½ **cups all-purpose flour**
 2 **teaspoons baking powder**
 ¼ **teaspoon salt**
  Gingercream (recipe follows)
 2 **pints fresh California strawberries,**
  stemmed and halved

Preheat oven to 350°F. Grease and flour 8-inch round cake pan. Beat butter in large bowl with electric mixer until creamy. Gradually add sugar, beating until well blended. Add ginger and eggs; beat well. Beat in combined dry ingredients alternately with ½ cup water. Spoon into prepared pan. Bake 45 minutes or until wooden pick inserted in center comes out clean. Cool in pan 5 minutes. Turn out onto rack to cool completely.

To assemble, slice cake in half horizontally. Place one layer on serving plate, cut side up. Spread with half of Gingercream; top with one fourth of the strawberries. Top with second cake layer, cut side down. Spoon remaining Gingercream over top; garnish with one fourth of the strawberries. Cut cake into wedges; serve with remaining strawberries. *Makes 8 servings*

Gingercream: Beat 1 cup whipping cream, 1 teaspoon granulated sugar and 1 teaspoon ground ginger in medium bowl with electric mixer until soft peaks form.

Favorite recipe from **California Strawberry Commission**

No-Bake Cherry Chocolate Shortcake

- 1   frozen loaf pound cake (10¾ ounces), thawed
- 1   can (21 ounces) cherry pie filling, chilled
- ⅓   cup HERSHEY¦S Cocoa or HERSHEY®S European Style Cocoa
- ½   cup powdered sugar
- 1   container (8 ounces) frozen non-dairy whipped topping, thawed (3½ cups)

Slice pound cake horizontally into three layers. Place bottom cake layer on serving plate; top with half the pie filling, using mostly cherries. Repeat with middle cake layer and remaining pie filling; place rounded layer on top. Cover; refrigerate several hours. Sift cocoa and powdered sugar onto whipped topping; stir until mixture is blended and smooth. Immediately spread over top and sides of cake, covering completely. Refrigerate leftover shortcake.

Makes about 6 servings

Chocolate-Apricot Crunch Torte

- 1 **frozen pound cake (16 ounces), thawed**
- 1 **pint whipping cream**
- ⅓ **cup unsweetened cocoa powder**
- ⅓ **cup sugar**
- 1 **package (6 ounces) HEATH® Bits, divided**
- 2 **tablespoons apricot preserves**
- 1 **tablespoon apricot brandy (optional)**

Slice cake lengthwise into three equal layers; set aside. In large bowl, combine cream, cocoa and sugar. Beat with electric mixer on high speed until stiff. Reserve ¼ cup HEATH® Bits; fold remaining into cream mixture. Refrigerate for 15 minutes. Meanwhile, in small saucepan over low heat, melt preserves. Stir in brandy, if desired.

Place bottom cake layer, cut side up, on serving plate. Brush half the preserve mixture over top of cake layer. Top with about ¾ cup whipped cream mixture, spreading to edges. Top with middle cake layer. Brush top with remaining preserve mixture; top with ¾ cup whipped cream mixture, spreading to edges. Top with remaining cake layer, cut side down. Spread remaining whipped cream mixture over top and sides of cake. Sprinkle with reserved HEATH® Bits; refrigerate 1 to 3 hours before serving. Cut into ¾-inch slices; garnish as desired. *Makes 10 servings*

Angel Food Cake with Pineapple Sauce

1 can (20 ounces) DOLE® Crushed
    Pineapple
1 tablespoon orange marmalade or peach
    fruit spread
2 tablespoons sugar
1 tablespoon cornstarch
1 prepared angel food cake

• **Combine** undrained pineapple, orange marmalade,
sugar and cornstarch in small saucepan. Bring to boil.
Reduce heat to low; cook 2 minutes, stirring
constantly, or until sauce thickens. Cool slightly. Sauce
can be served either warm or chilled.

• **Cut** cake into 12 slices. To serve, spoon sauce over
each slice.   *Makes 12 servings*

Mini Morsel Pound Cake

3 cups all-purpose flour
1 teaspoon baking powder
½ teaspoon salt
2 cups granulated sugar
1 cup (2 sticks) butter or margarine,
  softened
1 tablespoon vanilla extract
4 eggs
¾ cup milk
2 cups (12-ounce package) NESTLÉ®
  TOLL HOUSE® Semi-Sweet
  Chocolate Mini Morsels
  Powdered sugar

COMBINE flour, baking powder and salt in small bowl.
Beat sugar, butter and vanilla in large mixer bowl until
blended. Beat in eggs one at a time, beating well after
each addition. Gradually beat in flour mixture
alternately with milk. Stir in morsels. Pour into
greased and floured 10-inch bundt pan or two greased
and floured 9×5-inch loaf pans.

BAKE in preheated 325°F. oven for 65 to 75 minutes or
until wooden pick inserted near center comes out
clean. Cool in pan on wire rack for 15 minutes.
Remove from pan; serve warm or cool completely on
wire rack. Sprinkle with powdered sugar before
serving. *Makes 16 servings*

Apple-Streusel Pound Cake

  3   cups all-purpose flour
  ⅓   cup cornmeal
1½   teaspoons baking soda
1½   teaspoons baking powder
  ½   teaspoon salt
  1   cup granulated sugar
  1   cup skim milk
  1   cup nonfat sour cream
  ½   cup MOTT'S® Natural Apple Sauce
  1   whole egg
  2   tablespoons vegetable oil
  2   teaspoons vanilla extract
  3   egg whites, beaten until stiff
  ¾   cup firmly packed light brown sugar
  ¾   cup peeled, chopped apple
  ½   cup uncooked rolled oats
  2   teaspoons ground cinnamon

1. Preheat oven to 350°F. Spray 10-inch (12-cup) Bundt pan with nonstick cooking spray; flour lightly.

2. In medium bowl, combine flour, cornmeal, baking soda, baking powder and salt.

3. In large bowl, combine granulated sugar, milk, sour cream, apple sauce, whole egg, oil and vanilla.

4. Add flour mixture to apple sauce mixture; stir until well blended. Gently fold in beaten egg whites.

5. In small bowl, combine brown sugar, apple, oats and cinnamon.

6. Spread half of batter into prepared pan; sprinkle with oat mixture. Spread remaining batter over oat mixture.

7. Bake 60 to 70 minutes or until toothpick inserted in center comes out clean. Cool on wire rack 15 minutes before removing from pan. Place cake, fluted side up, on serving plate. Serve warm or cool completely. Cut into 24 slices.   *Makes 24 servings*

Raspberry Crown Cake

- 1 **package DUNCAN HINES® Angel Food Cake Mix**
- ¼ **cup sugar**
- 1 **tablespoon cornstarch**
- 1 **package (12 ounces) frozen dry pack red raspberries, thawed, drained and juice reserved**

1. Preheat oven to 350°F. Prepare, bake and cool cake following package directions.

2. Combine sugar and cornstarch in small saucepan. Stir in raspberry juice. Cook and stir on medium heat until mixture comes to a boil and is clear. Remove from heat; add raspberries. Cool slightly. Pour over top of cake and let run down sides. Refrigerate leftovers.
                                      Makes 12 to 16 servings

Peanut Butter Chip Pound Cake with Streusel Swirl

Streusel Swirl (recipe follows)
¾ cup (1½ sticks) butter or margarine, softened
1½ cups sugar
3 eggs
1 teaspoon vanilla extract
3 cups all-purpose flour
1½ teaspoons baking powder
1½ teaspoons baking soda
¼ teaspoon salt
1½ cups dairy sour cream
1⅔ cups (10-ounce package) REESE'S® Peanut Butter Chips
Peanut Butter Creme Glaze (recipe follows)

Prepare Streusel Swirl. Heat oven to 350°F. Grease 12-cup fluted tube pan. In large bowl, beat butter, sugar, eggs and vanilla until light and fluffy. Stir together flour, baking powder, baking soda and salt; add alternately with sour cream to butter mixture, beating well after each addition. Stir in peanut butter chips. Spread half the batter into prepared pan. Sprinkle Streusel Swirl over batter. Carefully spread remaining batter over top. Bake 1 hour 5 minutes to

1 hour 10 minutes or until top is golden brown and wooden pick inserted in center comes out clean. Cool 15 minutes; remove from pan to wire rack. Cool completely. Prepare Peanut Butter Creme Glaze; drizzle over cake. Garnish as desired.

Makes 10 to 12 servings

Streusel Swirl

¼ **cup packed brown sugar**
¼ **cup chopped nuts**
½ **teaspoon ground cinnamon**

In small bowl, stir together brown sugar, nuts and cinnamon.

Peanut Butter Creme Glaze

⅓ **cup sugar**
¼ **cup water**
1 **cup REESE'S® Peanut Butter Chips**
2 **tablespoons marshmallow creme**

In small saucepan, heat sugar and water until mixture comes to a boil. Remove from heat. Immediately add peanut butter chips; stir until melted. Add marshmallow creme; beat until smooth and of desired consistency. Add additional hot water, 1 teaspoon at a time, if needed.

Bittersweet Chocolate Pound Cake

CAKE
2   cups all-purpose flour
1   teaspoon baking soda
1   teaspoon baking powder
1½ cups water
2   tablespoons freeze dried coffee
4   bars (8 ounces) NESTLÉ® TOLL
        HOUSE® Unsweetened Baking
        Chocolate, broken into pieces, *divided*
2   cups granulated sugar
1   cup (2 sticks) butter, softened
1   teaspoon vanilla extract
3   eggs

CHOCOLATE GLAZE
3   tablespoons butter or margarine
1½ cups sifted powdered sugar
2   to 3 tablespoons water
1   teaspoon vanilla extract
    Powdered sugar (optional)

FOR CAKE:
COMBINE flour, baking soda and baking powder in small bowl. Bring water and coffee to a boil in small saucepan; remove from heat. Add *3 bars (6 ounces)* baking chocolate; stir until smooth.

BEAT sugar, butter and vanilla in large mixer bowl until creamy. Add eggs; beat on high speed for 5 minutes. Beat in flour mixture alternately with chocolate mixture. Pour into well-greased 10-inch bundt pan.

BAKE in preheated 325°F. oven for 50 to 60 minutes or until long wooden pick inserted near center comes out clean. Cool in pan on wire rack for 30 minutes. Invert onto wire rack; cool completely. Drizzle with chocolate glaze; sprinkle with powdered sugar.

FOR CHOCOLATE GLAZE:
MELT *remaining* baking bar (2 ounces) and butter in small, heavy saucepan over low heat, stirring until smooth. Remove from heat. Stir in powdered sugar alternately with water until of desired consistency. Stir in vanilla. *Makes 12 servings*

Marble Chiffon Cake

- 2 **tablespoons plus 1½ cups sugar, divided**
- 2 **tablespoons plus ½ cup vegetable oil, divided**
- ⅓ **cup HERSHEY₂S Cocoa**
- 1 **cup cold water, divided**
- 2 **cups all-purpose flour**
- 1 **tablespoon baking powder**
- 1 **teaspoon salt**
- 7 **eggs, separated**
- 2 **teaspoons vanilla extract**
- ½ **teaspoon cream of tartar**
     Vanilla Glaze or Quick Cocoa Glaze (recipes follow)

Preheat oven to 325°F. In small bowl, combine
2 tablespoons sugar, 2 tablespoons oil, cocoa and ¼ cup
cold water; stir until smooth. Reserve. In medium
bowl, stir together flour, remaining 1½ cups sugar,
baking powder and salt. Add remaining ¾ cup cold
water, ½ cup oil, egg yolks and vanilla. Beat on low
speed of electric mixer until combined; continue
beating on high speed 5 minutes. In large bowl, with
clean set of beaters, beat egg whites with cream of
tartar until stiff peaks form. Pour batter in thin stream
over beaten whites, gently folding with rubber spatula
just until blended. Remove one third of batter to
separate bowl; gently fold in reserved cocoa mixture.
Pour half of light batter into ungreased 10-inch tube
pan; top with half of chocolate batter. Repeat layers.
With spatula or knife, swirl gently through batters to
marbleize.

Bake 65 to 70 minutes or until top springs back when touched lightly. Invert pan on heatproof funnel or bottle; cool cake completely. Loosen cake from pan; invert onto serving plate. Spread Vanilla Glaze or Quick Cocoa Glaze over top of cake, allowing glaze to drizzle down sides.   *Makes 12 to 16 servings*

Vanilla Glaze: In small saucepan over low heat, melt ¼ cup butter or margarine; remove from heat. Gradually stir in 2 cups powdered sugar, 2 to 3 tablespoons hot water and 1 teaspoon vanilla extract; beat with wire whisk until smooth and slightly thickened.

Quick Cocoa Glaze

>   2 tablespoons butter or margarine
> ¼ cup HERSHEY₀S Cocoa
>   3 tablespoons water
> ½ teaspoon vanilla extract
> 1¼ cups powdered sugar

In small saucepan over low heat, melt butter. Stir in cocoa and water. Cook, stirring constantly, until mixture thickens. *Do not boil.* Remove from heat. Stir in vanilla. Gradually add powdered sugar, beating with wire whisk until smooth. Add additional water, ½ teaspoon at a time, until desired consistency.

Bumpy Highway Cake

CAKE

- 1 can (14 ounces) sweetened condensed milk (not evaporated), divided
- 1 BUTTER FLAVOR* CRISCO® Stick or 1 cup BUTTER FLAVOR CRISCO all-vegetable shortening
- 1 cup granulated sugar
- 1 cup firmly packed light brown sugar
- 4 eggs
- 2 teaspoons vanilla
- 1 cup buttermilk or sour milk**
- ½ cup unsweetened baking cocoa
- 2½ cups all-purpose flour
- 1 teaspoon baking soda
- 1 teaspoon ground cinnamon
- ½ teaspoon salt
- 1 cup hot water

DRIZZLE

- ⅓ cup unsweetened baking cocoa***
- 3 tablespoons CRISCO® Oil or CRISCO® PURITAN® Canola Oil

FROSTING

- ¼ BUTTER FLAVOR CRISCO Stick or ¼ cup BUTTER FLAVOR CRISCO all-vegetable shortening
- 1 cup confectioners' sugar
- ½ cup miniature marshmallows, halved
- 1 cup chopped nuts

1. Heat oven to 350°F. **Grease** 10-inch (12-cup) Bundt pan with shortening. **Flour** lightly.

2. Measure ⅓ cup condensed milk for cake. **Reserve** remaining milk for frosting.

3. For Cake, combine 1 cup shortening, granulated sugar, brown sugar, eggs, ⅓ cup condensed milk and vanilla in large bowl. **Beat** at medium speed of electric mixer until creamy. **Add** buttermilk and ½ cup cocoa. **Beat** until well blended.

4. Combine flour, baking soda, cinnamon and salt in medium bowl. **Add** to creamed mixture. **Beat** at low speed to blend. **Beat** at medium speed 5 minutes. **Stir** in hot water with spoon just until blended. *Do not overmix.* (Batter will be thin.) **Pour** into pan.

5. Bake at 350°F for 35 to 50 minutes or until top springs back when touched lightly in center or until toothpick inserted in center comes out clean. **Cool** 5 minutes before removing from pan. **Place** cake, fluted side up, on serving plate. **Cool** 15 minutes.

6. For Drizzle, combine ⅓ cup cocoa and oil in small bowl. **Stir** to blend.

7. For Frosting, combine ¼ cup shortening, reserved condensed milk and confectioners' sugar in medium bowl. **Beat** at high speed until glossy. **Spread** on warm cake. **Sprinkle** with marshmallows and then nuts. **Decorate** with chocolate drizzle. **Serve** warm or cool completely.   *Makes 12 to 16 servings*

*Butter Flavor Crisco is artificially flavored.

**To sour milk: Combine 1 tablespoon white vinegar plus enough milk to equal 1 cup. Stir. Wait 5 minutes before using.

***Substitute 4 bars (1 ounce each) unsweetened baking chocolate, melted, for cocoa and oil, if desired.

Chocolate-Chocolate Cake

1 package (8 ounces) PHILADELPHIA
   BRAND® Cream Cheese, softened
1 cup BREAKSTONE'S® or KNUDSEN®
   Sour Cream
½ cup coffee-flavored liqueur or water
2 eggs
1 package (2-layer size) chocolate cake
   mix
1 package (4-serving size) JELL-O®
   Chocolate Flavor Instant Pudding
   and Pie Filling
1 cup BAKER'S® Semi-Sweet Real
   Chocolate Chips

MIX cream cheese, sour cream, liqueur and eggs with
electric mixer on medium speed until well blended.
Add cake mix and pudding mix; beat until well blended.
Fold in chips. (Batter will be stiff.)

POUR into greased and floured 12-cup fluted tube pan.

BAKE at 325°F for 1 hour to 1 hour and 5 minutes or
until toothpick inserted near center comes out clean.
Cool 5 minutes. Remove from pan. Cool completely on
wire rack. Sprinkle with powdered sugar before
serving. Garnish, if desired.

Makes 10 to 12 servings

Classic HERSHEY® Bar Cake

 1   cup (2 sticks) butter or margarine,
       softened
1¼   cups granulated sugar
 4   eggs
 6   HERSHEY'S Milk Chocolate Bars
       (1.55 ounces each), melted
2½   cups all-purpose flour
 ¼   teaspoon baking soda
       Dash salt
 1   cup buttermilk or sour milk*
 ½   cup HERSHEY'S Syrup
 2   teaspoons vanilla extract
 1   cup chopped pecans
       Powdered sugar (optional)

Heat oven to 350°F. Grease and flour 10-inch tube pan
or 12-cup fluted tube pan. In large bowl, beat butter
until creamy; gradually add granulated sugar, beating
on medium speed of electric mixer until well blended.
Add eggs, one at a time, beating well after each
addition. Add chocolate; beat until blended. Stir
together flour, baking soda and salt; add to chocolate
mixture alternately with buttermilk, beating until
blended. Add syrup and vanilla; beat until blended. Stir
in pecans. Pour batter into prepared pan. Bake 1 hour
and 15 minutes or until wooden pick inserted in center
of cake comes out clean. Cool 10 minutes; remove
from pan to wire rack. Cool completely. Sift powdered
sugar over top.   *Makes 12 to 16 servings*

*To sour milk, use 1 tablespoon white vinegar plus milk to equal
1 cup.

Cappuccino Cake

½ cup (3 ounces) semisweet chocolate
    chips
½ cup chopped hazelnuts, walnuts or
    pecans
1 (18.25-ounce) package yellow cake mix
¼ cup instant espresso coffee powder
2 teaspoons ground cinnamon
1¼ cups water
3 large eggs
⅓ cup FILIPPO BERIO® Pure or Extra
    Light Olive Oil
    Powdered sugar
1 (15-ounce) container ricotta cheese
2 teaspoons granulated sugar
    Additional ground cinnamon

Preheat oven to 325°F. Grease 10-inch (12-cup) Bundt
pan or 10-inch tube pan with olive oil. Sprinkle lightly
with flour.

In small bowl, combine chocolate chips and hazelnuts.
Spoon evenly onto bottom of prepared pan. In large
bowl, combine cake mix, coffee powder and
2 teaspoons cinnamon. Add water, eggs and olive oil.
Beat with electric mixer at low speed until dry
ingredients are moistened. Beat at medium speed
2 minutes. Pour batter over topping in pan.

Bake 60 minutes or until toothpick inserted in center
comes out clean. Cool on wire rack 15 minutes.
Remove from pan. Place cake, fluted side up, on
serving plate. Cool completely. Sprinkle with powdered

sugar. In medium bowl, combine ricotta cheese and granulated sugar. Sprinkle with cinnamon. Serve alongside slices of cake. Serve cake with cappuccino or coffee, if desired.   *Makes 12 to 16 servings*

Hot Fudge Pudding Cake

1¼   cups granulated sugar, divided
  1   cup all-purpose flour
  3   tablespoons plus ¼ cup HERSHEY₀S Cocoa, divided
  2   teaspoons baking powder
  ¼   teaspoon salt
  ½   cup milk
  ⅓   cup butter or margarine, melted
1½   teaspoons vanilla extract
  ½   cup packed light brown sugar
1¼   cups hot water
      Whipped topping (optional)

Heat oven to 350°F. In large bowl, stir together ¾ cup granulated sugar, flour, 3 tablespoons cocoa, baking powder and salt. Stir in milk, butter and vanilla; beat until smooth. Pour batter into 8- or 9-inch square baking pan. Stir together remaining ½ cup granulated sugar, brown sugar and remaining ¼ cup cocoa; sprinkle mixture evenly over batter. Pour water over top. *Do not stir.* Bake 35 to 40 minutes or until center is almost set. Cool 15 minutes; spoon into dessert dishes. Spoon sauce from bottom of pan over top of cake. Serve warm with whipped topping, if desired. Garnish as desired.   *Makes 8 servings*

Chocolate Raspberry Avalanche Cake

2 cups all-purpose flour
2 cups granulated sugar
6 tablespoons unsweetened cocoa
1½ teaspoons baking soda
1 teaspoon salt
1 cup hot coffee
¾ BUTTER FLAVOR* CRISCO® Stick or
   ¾ cup BUTTER FLAVOR CRISCO
   all-vegetable shortening
½ cup milk
3 eggs
¼ cup raspberry-flavored liqueur
   Confectioners sugar
1 cup fresh raspberries

*Butter Flavor Crisco is artificially flavored.

1. Heat oven to 350°F. **Grease** 10-inch (12-cup) Bundt pan with shortening. **Flour** lightly.

2. Combine flour, granulated sugar, cocoa, baking soda and salt in large bowl. **Add** coffee and shortening. **Beat** at low speed of electric mixer until dry ingredients are moistened. **Add** milk. **Beat** at medium speed 1½ minutes. **Add** eggs, 1 at a time, beating well after each addition. **Pour** into prepared pan.

3. Bake at 350°F for 40 to 45 minutes, or until toothpick inserted in center comes out clean. **Cool** 10 minutes before removing from pan. **Place** cake, fluted side up, on wire rack. **Cool** 10 minutes. **Brush** top and side with liqueur. **Cool** completely. **Dust** top with confectioners sugar.

4. Place cake on serving plate. **Fill** center with raspberries, if desired.

Makes one 10-inch cake (12 to 16 servings)

Citrus Crown Cake

1 jar (12 ounces) orange marmalade
⅔ cup flaked coconut
¼ cup butter or margarine, melted
1 package DUNCAN HINES® Moist
   Deluxe Lemon Supreme Cake Mix

1. Preheat oven to 350°F. Grease generously and flour 10-inch Bundt pan.

2. Combine marmalade, coconut and melted butter in small bowl. Pour into pan.

3. Prepare cake following package directions for Basic Recipe. Pour batter over marmalade mixture. Bake at 350°F for 50 to 55 minutes or until toothpick inserted in center comes out clean. Cool in pan 10 minutes. Invert cake onto serving plate. Cool completely.

Makes 12 to 16 servings

Tip: For best results, cut cake with a serrated knife; clean after each slice.

Luscious Key Lime Cake

CAKE
- 1 package DUNCAN HINES® Moist Deluxe Lemon Supreme Cake Mix
- 1 package (4-serving size) lemon instant pudding and pie filling mix
- 4 eggs
- 1 cup CRISCO® Oil or CRISCO® PURITAN® Canola Oil
- ¾ cup water
- ¼ cup Key lime juice (see Tip)

GLAZE
- 2 cups confectioners sugar
- ⅓ cup Key lime juice
- 2 tablespoons water
- 2 tablespoons butter or margarine, melted
  Additional confectioners sugar
  Lime slices, for garnish
  Fresh strawberry slices, for garnish (optional)

1. Preheat oven to 350°F. Grease and flour 10-inch Bundt pan.

2. For cake, combine cake mix, pudding mix, eggs, oil, ¾ cup water and ¼ cup Key lime juice in large bowl. Beat at low speed with electric mixer until moistened.

Beat at medium speed for 2 minutes. Pour into pan.
Bake at 350°F for 50 to 60 minutes or until toothpick
inserted in center comes out clean. Cool in pan
25 minutes. Invert onto cooling rack. Return cake to
pan. Poke holes in top of warm cake with toothpick or
long-tined fork.

3. For glaze, combine 2 cups confectioners sugar, ⅓
cup Key lime juice, 2 tablespoons water and melted
butter in medium bowl. Pour slowly over top of warm
cake. Cool completely. Invert onto serving plate. Dust
with additional confectioners sugar. Garnish with lime
slices and strawberry slices, if desired.

Makes 12 to 16 servings

Tip: Fresh or bottled lime juice may be substituted for
the Key lime juice.

Fresh Apple Cake

CAKE

- 1 package DUNCAN HINES® Moist Deluxe Yellow Cake Mix
- 3 eggs
- 1¼ cups apple juice
- ⅓ cup CRISCO® Oil or CRISCO® PURITAN® Canola Oil
- 1 teaspoon ground cinnamon
- 2 cups peeled, grated apples (about 2 medium)
- ½ cup all-purpose flour
- 1 cup chopped pecans

FROSTING

- 3 tablespoons butter or margarine
- 3 tablespoons granulated sugar
- 3 tablespoons brown sugar
- 3 tablespoons whipping cream
- ½ cup confectioners sugar
- ¼ teaspoon vanilla extract
  Pecan halves, for garnish

1. Preheat oven to 350°F. Grease and flour 10-inch tube pan.

2. For cake, combine cake mix, eggs, apple juice, oil and cinnamon in large bowl. Beat at medium speed with electric mixer for 2 minutes. Toss apples with flour in medium bowl. Fold flour-coated apples and

chopped pecans into batter. Pour into pan. Bake at
350°F for 45 minutes or until toothpick inserted in
center comes out clean. Cool in pan 25 minutes. Invert
onto serving plate. Cool completely.

3. For frosting, combine butter, granulated sugar,
brown sugar and whipping cream in small heavy
saucepan. Bring to a boil over medium heat; boil
1 minute. Remove from heat; cool 20 minutes. Add
confectioners sugar and vanilla extract; blend with
wooden spoon until smooth and thick. Spread frosting
on cake. Garnish with pecan halves.

Makes 12 to 16 servings

Tip: Apples may be grated in a food processor using the
shredding disc. If a food processor is not available, use
a hand grater.

Butter Pecan Banana Cake

CAKE

1 package DUNCAN HINES® Moist
  Deluxe Butter Recipe Golden
  Cake Mix
4 eggs
1 cup mashed, ripe bananas (about
  3 medium)
¾ cup CRISCO® Oil or CRISCO®
  PURITAN® Canola Oil
½ cup sugar
¼ cup milk
1 teaspoon vanilla extract
1 cup chopped pecans

FROSTING

1 cup coarsely chopped pecans
¼ cup butter or margarine
1 container (16 ounces) DUNCAN
  HINES® Creamy Homestyle Vanilla
  Frosting

1. Preheat oven to 325°F. Grease and flour 10-inch
Bundt or tube pan.

2. For cake, combine cake mix, eggs, bananas, oil,
sugar, milk and vanilla extract in large bowl. Beat at
low speed with electric mixer until moistened. Beat at
medium speed for 2 minutes. Stir in 1 cup chopped
pecans. Pour into prepared pan. Bake at 325°F for 50 to
60 minutes or until toothpick inserted in center comes
out clean. Cool in pan 25 minutes. Invert onto cooling
rack. Cool completely.

3. For frosting, place 1 cup coarsely chopped pecans and butter in skillet. Cook on medium heat, stirring until pecans are toasted. Stir into frosting. Cool until spreading consistency. Frost cake.

Makes 12 to 16 servings

Applesauce Walnut Cake

   1   package DUNCAN HINES® Moist
         Deluxe Butter Recipe Golden
         Cake Mix
   3   eggs
 1⅓   cups applesauce
   ½   cup butter or margarine, melted
   1   teaspoon ground cinnamon
   ½   cup chopped walnuts
         Confectioners sugar, for garnish

1. Preheat oven to 375°F. Grease and flour 10-inch Bundt or tube pan.

2. Combine cake mix, eggs, applesauce, melted butter and cinnamon in large bowl. Beat at low speed with electric mixer until moistened. Beat at medium speed for 4 minutes. Stir in walnuts. Pour into pan. Bake at 375°F for 45 to 55 minutes or until toothpick inserted in center comes out clean. Cool in pan 25 minutes. Invert cake onto serving plate. Cool completely. Dust with confectioners sugar.

Makes 12 to 16 servings

Tip: Also delicious using chopped pecans instead of walnuts.

Sock-It-To-Me Cake

STREUSEL FILLING
- 1 **package DUNCAN HINES® Moist Deluxe Butter Recipe Golden Cake Mix, divided**
- 2 **tablespoons brown sugar**
- 2 **teaspoons ground cinnamon**
- 1 **cup finely chopped pecans**

CAKE
- 4 **eggs**
- 1 **cup dairy sour cream**
- ⅓ **cup CRISCO® Oil or CRISCO® PURITAN® Canola Oil**
- ¼ **cup water**
- ¼ **cup granulated sugar**

GLAZE
- 1 **cup confectioners sugar**
- 1 **or 2 tablespoons milk**

1. Preheat oven to 375°F. Grease and flour 10-inch tube pan.

2. For streusel filling, combine 2 tablespoons cake mix, brown sugar and cinnamon in medium bowl. Stir in pecans. Set aside.

3. For cake, combine remaining cake mix, eggs, sour cream, oil, water and granulated sugar in large bowl. Beat at medium speed with electric mixer for 2 minutes. Pour two thirds of batter into pan. Sprinkle with streusel filling. Spoon remaining batter evenly over filling. Bake at 375°F for 45 to 55 minutes or until toothpick inserted in center comes out clean. Cool in pan 25 minutes. Invert onto serving plate. Cool completely.

4. For glaze, combine confectioners sugar and milk in small bowl. Stir until smooth. Drizzle over cake.

Makes 12 to 16 servings

Tip: For a quick glaze, heat ½ cup DUNCAN HINES® Creamy Homestyle Vanilla Frosting in small saucepan over medium heat, stirring constantly, until thin.

Spicy Butterscotch Snack Cake

1 cup (2 sticks) butter or margarine,
 softened
1 cup sugar
2 eggs
½ teaspoon vanilla extract
½ cup applesauce
2½ cups all-purpose flour
1½ to 2 teaspoons ground cinnamon
1 teaspoon baking soda
½ teaspoon salt
1⅔ cups (10-ounce package) HERSHEY'S
 Butterscotch Chips
1 cup chopped pecans (optional)
 Powdered sugar or frozen non-dairy
 whipped topping, thawed (optional)

Heat oven to 350°F. Lightly grease 13×9×2-inch
baking pan. In large bowl, beat butter and sugar until
light and fluffy. Add eggs and vanilla; beat well. Mix in
applesauce. Stir together flour, cinnamon, baking soda
and salt; gradually add to butter mixture, beating until
well blended. Stir in butterscotch chips and pecans, if
desired. Spread into prepared pan. Bake 35 to 40
minutes or until wooden pick inserted in center comes
out clean. Cool completely in pan on wire rack.
Sprinkle with powdered sugar or serve with whipped
topping, if desired. *Makes 12 servings*

Cocoa Marble Gingerbread

½ cup shortening
1 cup sugar
1 cup light molasses
2 eggs
1 teaspoon baking soda
1 cup boiling water
2 cups all-purpose flour
1 teaspoon salt
¼ cup HERSHEY'S Cocoa
½ teaspoon ground cinnamon
½ teaspoon ground ginger
¼ teaspoon ground cloves
¼ teaspoon ground nutmeg
Sweetened whipped cream (optional)

Heat oven to 350°F. Grease and flour 13×9×2-inch
baking pan. In large bowl, beat shortening, sugar and
molasses until blended. Add eggs; beat well. Stir baking
soda into water to dissolve; add to shortening mixture
alternately with combined flour and salt, beating well
after each addition. Remove 2 cups batter to medium
bowl. Add cocoa; blend well. Add spices to remaining
batter in large bowl. Alternately spoon batters into
prepared pan; gently swirl with knife for marbled
effect. Bake 40 to 45 minutes or until wooden pick
inserted in center comes out clean. Serve warm or at
room temperature with sweetened whipped cream,
if desired.   *Makes 10 to 12 servings*

Easy Carrot Cake

½ cup Prune Purée (recipe follows)
2 cups all-purpose flour
2 teaspoons ground cinnamon
1½ teaspoons baking soda
½ teaspoon salt
4 cups shredded DOLE® Carrots
2 cups sugar
½ cup DOLE® Pineapple Juice
2 eggs
2 teaspoons vanilla extract
Vegetable cooking spray

• **Prepare** prune purée; set aside.

• **Combine** flour, cinnamon, baking soda and salt in medium bowl; set aside.

• **Beat** together prune purée, carrots, sugar, juice, eggs and vanilla in large bowl until blended. Add flour mixture; stir until well blended.

• **Spread** batter into 13×9-inch baking dish sprayed with vegetable cooking spray.

• **Bake** at 375°F 30 to 35 minutes or until toothpick inserted in center comes out clean. Cool completely in dish on wire rack. Dust with powdered sugar; garnish with carrot curls, if desired. *Makes 12 servings*

Prune Purée: Combine 1⅓ cups DOLE® Pitted Prunes, halved, and ½ cup hot water in food processor or blender. Process until prunes are finely chopped, stopping to scrape down sides occasionally. (Purée can be refrigerated in airtight container for up to 1 week.)

Pineapple Upside-Down Cake

1   (8-ounce) can crushed pineapple in
     juice, undrained
2   tablespoons margarine, melted, divided
½   cup firmly packed light brown sugar
6   whole maraschino cherries, halved
1½ cups all-purpose flour
2   tablespoons baking powder
¼   teaspoon salt
1   cup granulated sugar
½   cup MOTT'S® Natural Apple Sauce
1   whole egg
3   egg whites, beaten until stiff

1. Preheat oven to 375°F. Drain pineapple; reserve
juice. Spray sides of 8-inch square baking pan with
nonstick cooking spray.

2. Spread 1 tablespoon melted margarine in bottom of
prepared pan. Sprinkle with brown sugar; top with
pineapple. Arrange cherries, cut side up, so that when
cake is cut, each piece will have cherry half in center.

3. In small bowl, combine flour, baking powder and
salt. In large bowl, combine granulated sugar, apple
sauce, whole egg, remaining 1 tablespoon melted
margarine and reserved pineapple juice.

4. Add flour mixture to apple sauce mixture; stir until
well blended. Fold in egg whites. Gently pour batter
over fruit, spreading evenly.

5. Bake 35 to 40 minutes or until lightly browned.
Cool on wire rack 10 minutes. Invert cake onto serving
plate. Serve warm or cool.   *Makes 12 servings*

Light and Luscious Lemon Cake

1 package DUNCAN HINES® Moist
   Deluxe Lemon Supreme Cake Mix

FROSTING

1 can (6 ounces) frozen lemonade
   concentrate, thawed

1 can (14 ounces) sweetened condensed
   milk

1 container (8 ounces) frozen whipped
   topping, thawed

3 drops yellow food coloring (optional)
   Lemon slices, for garnish

1. Preheat oven to 350°F. Grease and flour
13×9×2-inch pan.

2. Prepare and bake cake following package directions.
Cool in pan 15 minutes. Invert onto cooling rack. Cool
completely. Split cake in half horizontally. Set aside.

3. For frosting, combine lemonade concentrate and
sweetened condensed milk in medium bowl. Fold in
whipped topping. Add food coloring, if desired. Blend
well. Place bottom cut cake layer on serving plate.
Spread one-third frosting on top. Place second cake
layer on top of frosting. Frost sides and top with
remaining frosting. Garnish with lemon slices.
Refrigerate until ready to serve.

Makes 12 to 16 servings

Tip: To cut cake evenly, measure cake with ruler.
Divide into 2 equal layers. Mark with toothpicks. Cut
through layer with large serrated knife using
toothpicks as guide.

Mississippi NILLA® Mud Cake

1½ cups margarine
4 eggs
1 cup unsweetened cocoa
1½ cups all-purpose flour
2 cups granulated sugar
¼ teaspoon salt
1¼ cups PLANTERS® Pecans, chopped
3 cups miniature marshmallows
35 NILLA® Wafers
1 (1-pound) box powdered sugar
½ cup milk
½ teaspoon vanilla extract

Preheat oven to 350°F. In large bowl, with electric mixer at medium speed, beat 1 cup margarine, eggs and ½ cup cocoa until well combined. Blend in flour, granulated sugar, salt and pecans. Spread batter in greased 13×9×2-inch baking pan. Bake at 350°F for 30 to 35 minutes or until cake pulls away from sides of pan.

Sprinkle marshmallows over hot cake; return to oven for 2 minutes or until marshmallows are slightly puffed. Arrange wafers over marshmallow layer.

In medium bowl, with electric mixer at medium speed, beat remaining ½ cup margarine, confectioner's sugar, remaining ½ cup cocoa, milk and vanilla until smooth; spread immediately over wafer layer. Cool cake completely on wire rack. Cut into squares to serve.

Makes 24 servings

Frosted Peanut Butter Cake Squares

About 30 REESE'S® Peanut Butter
  Cup Miniatures
⅓ cup butter or margarine, softened
½ cup REESE'S® Creamy or Crunchy
  Peanut Butter
⅓ cup granulated sugar
⅓ cup packed light brown sugar
½ cup milk
2 eggs
1 teaspoon vanilla extract
1 cup all-purpose flour
1 teaspoon baking soda
¼ teaspoon salt
Chocolate Peanut Butter Topping
  (recipe follows)

Heat oven to 350°F. Remove wrappers from candies.
Chop candies into pieces. Grease 13×9×2-inch baking
pan. In medium bowl, beat butter, peanut butter,
granulated sugar and brown sugar until well blended.
Gradually add milk, eggs and vanilla, beating until
smooth and well blended. Stir together flour, baking
soda and salt. Add to butter mixture; beat until well
blended. Spread batter into prepared pan. Bake 18 to
20 minutes or until wooden pick inserted in center

comes out clean. Cool completely in pan on wire rack.
Prepare Chocolate Peanut Butter Topping; spread over
cake. Sprinkle candy pieces over top. Cut into squares.

Makes 12 to 14 squares

Chocolate Peanut Butter Topping

½ cup HERSHEY₅S Semi-Sweet
    Chocolate Chips
⅓ cup REESE'S₅ Creamy Peanut Butter
2 tablespoons butter or margarine
¼ cup powdered sugar

In medium microwave-safe bowl, place chocolate
chips, peanut butter and butter. Microwave at HIGH
(100%) 1 minute; stir. If necessary, microwave at HIGH
an additional 15 seconds at a time, stirring after each
addition, just until chips are melted when stirred. Add
powdered sugar; whisk until smooth and of spreading
consistency.

Pecan Fudge Sheetcake

1   **package DUNCAN HINES® Moist
    Deluxe Devil's Food Cake Mix**
½   **cup butter or margarine**
¼   **cup plus 2 tablespoons milk**
¼   **cup unsweetened cocoa**
1   **pound confectioners sugar (3½ to
    4 cups)**
1   **teaspoon vanilla extract**
¾   **cup chopped pecans**

1. Preheat oven to 350°F. Grease 15½×10½×1-inch jelly-roll pan.

2. Prepare cake following package directions. Pour into pan. Bake at 350°F for 20 to 25 minutes or until toothpick inserted in center comes out clean.

3. For frosting, place butter, milk and cocoa in medium saucepan. Stir on low heat until butter is melted. Add confectioners sugar and vanilla extract, stirring until smooth. Stir in pecans. Pour over warm cake. Cool completely.   *Makes 20 servings*

Tip: For best results, allow the cake to cool undisturbed until frosting is set, about 4 hours.

Light & Luscious Chocolate Cake with Raspberry Sauce

2   cups all-purpose flour
1⅓ cups skim milk
1   cup sugar
1   cup EGG BEATERS® Healthy Real Egg
     Product
⅔   cup unsweetened cocoa
⅔   cup margarine, softened
1½ teaspoons baking powder
1½ teaspoons vanilla extract
½   teaspoon baking soda
     Raspberry Sauce (recipe follows)
     Fresh raspberries and fresh mint
        sprigs, for garnish

In large bowl, with electric mixer at medium speed,
combine flour, milk, sugar, EGG BEATERS®, cocoa,
margarine, baking powder, vanilla and baking soda just
until blended. Beat at high speed for 3 minutes. Spread
batter into lightly greased 13×9×2-inch baking pan.
Bake at 350°F for 30 to 35 minutes or until toothpick
inserted in center comes out clean. Cool in pan on wire
rack. Cut into 16 (3×2-inch) pieces. Serve topped with
Raspberry Sauce. Garnish with raspberries and mint.

Makes 16 servings

Raspberry Sauce: In electric blender container, purée
2 cups thawed frozen raspberries in syrup; strain. Stir
in 2 tablespoons sugar and 1 tablespoon cornstarch.
In small saucepan, cook raspberry mixture until
thickened and boiling. Cover; chill.

Chocolate Cake with Almond Frosting

1 tablespoon instant coffee granules
1 cup boiling water
1 cup unsweetened cocoa powder
2 cups all-purpose flour
2 cups sugar
2 teaspoons baking soda
1 teaspoon baking powder
¼ teaspoon salt
1 cup skim milk
3 jars (2½ ounces each) puréed prunes
4 egg whites
1 tablespoon vanilla extract
½ teaspoon almond extract
   Almond Frosting (recipe follows)
¼ cup sliced toasted almonds (optional)

1. Preheat oven to 350°F. Spray 13×9×2-inch baking pan with nonstick cooking spray.

2. Combine coffee granules and boiling water in measuring cup. Stir until coffee is completely dissolved. Set aside.

3. Sift cocoa into large bowl. Add flour, sugar, baking soda, baking powder and salt; mix well. In another large bowl, combine coffee, milk, prunes, egg whites, vanilla and almond extracts; mix well. Add coffee mixture to cocoa mixture; mix well.

4. Pour batter into prepared pan. Bake 30 minutes or until wooden pick inserted in center of cake comes out clean. Cool in pan on wire rack 10 minutes. Invert onto serving plate; cool completely.

5. Prepare Almond Frosting; frost cake. Garnish with toasted almonds, if desired.   *Makes 12 servings*

Almond Frosting

   3   **egg whites***
1½   **cups firmly packed light brown sugar**
  ¼   **cup water**
   1   **teaspoon cream of tartar**
   2   **teaspoons vanilla extract**
   1   **teaspoon almond extract**

1. Combine egg whites, brown sugar, water and cream of tartar in top of double boiler. Place over simmering water. Using electric hand mixer, beat until stiff peaks form, about 5 minutes.

2. Add vanilla and almond extracts; beat 2 minutes. Remove from heat; cool.

*Use only clean, uncracked Grade A eggs.

Low Fat Devil's Chocolate Fudge Cake

CAKE

    1   cup water
    ½   cup Prune Purée (recipe follows) or
         prepared prune butter
    3   egg whites
  1½ teaspoons vanilla
    1   cup plus 2 tablespoons all-purpose
         flour
    1   cup plus 2 tablespoons granulated
         sugar
    ¾   cup unsweetened cocoa powder
  1½ teaspoons baking powder
    ¼   teaspoon baking soda
    ¼   teaspoon salt

ICING

  2½ cups powdered sugar
    ¼   cup unsweetened cocoa powder
    ¼   cup low fat (1%) milk
        Fresh raspberries and mint sprig, for
        garnish

Preheat oven to 350°F. Coat 9-inch square baking pan
with vegetable cooking spray. To make cake, in mixer
bowl, beat water, prune purée, egg whites and vanilla

until well blended. Add flour, granulated sugar, ¾ cup cocoa, baking powder, baking soda and salt; mix well. Spread batter evenly in prepared pan. Bake in center of oven about 30 minutes until pick inserted into center comes out clean. Cool completely in pan on wire rack.

To make icing, in small mixer bowl, beat powdered sugar, ¼ cup cocoa and milk until smooth. Spread on cake. Garnish with raspberries and mint. Cut cake into 3-inch squares.   *Makes 9 servings*

Prune Purée: Combine 1⅓ cups (8 ounces) pitted prunes and 6 tablespoons hot water in container of food processor or blender. Pulse on and off until prunes are finely chopped and smooth. Store leftovers in a covered container in the refrigerator for up to two months. Makes 1 cup.

Tip: Unsweetened cocoa powder provides rich chocolate flavor with less fat than other baking chocolates because most of the cocoa butter has been removed.

Favorite recipe from **California Prune Board**

Easy Boston Cream Pie

½ package light yellow cake mix
⅛ teaspoon baking soda
⅔ cup water
2 egg whites
1½ teaspoons vanilla, divided
1 package (3⅜ ounces) sugar-free instant
   vanilla pudding mix
1⅓ cups skim milk
Chocolate Glaze (recipe follows)

1. Preheat oven to 350°F. Spray 9-inch round cake pan with nonstick cooking spray. Lightly coat with flour. Set aside.

2. Combine cake mix and baking soda in large bowl; mix well. Add water, egg whites and 1 teaspoon vanilla. Using electric mixer, beat on low speed 30 seconds. Increase speed to medium; beat 2 minutes.

3. Pour batter into prepared pan. Bake 30 minutes or until cake pulls away from side of pan and springs back when touched lightly in center. Remove from oven. Cool 10 minutes on wire rack. Invert onto serving plate; cool completely.

4. Combine pudding mix, milk and remaining ½ teaspoon vanilla in medium bowl. Using electric mixer, beat on low speed 2 minutes. Set aside.

5. Prepare Chocolate Glaze.

6. Cut cake in half horizontally; carefully remove top half of cake. Spread bottom half with pudding mixture. Replace top half; spoon Chocolate Glaze over top. Allow to stand until Glaze hardens. Cut into wedges.

Makes 8 servings

Chocolate Glaze

⅔ **cup powdered sugar**
1 **tablespoon unsweetened cocoa powder**
1 **tablespoon water**
½ **teaspoon vanilla extract**

1. Sift together powdered sugar and cocoa in medium bowl. Add water and vanilla; mix well.

2. Add more water until desired spreading consistency.

Boston Cream Pie

CAKE
- 2¼ cups cake flour
- 2 teaspoons baking powder
- 1 teaspoon salt
- ½ teaspoon baking soda
- 1½ cups granulated sugar
- 2 tablespoons margarine, softened
- ½ cup MOTT'S® Natural Apple Sauce
- ½ cup skim milk
- 4 egg whites
- 1 teaspoon vanilla extract

FILLING
- 1 (0.9-ounce) package sugar-free instant vanilla pudding
- 1½ cups skim milk

CHOCOLATE GLAZE
- 1½ cups powdered sugar
- 2 tablespoons unsweetened cocoa powder
- 1 tablespoon skim milk
- ½ teaspoon vanilla extract
- Lemon peel strips (optional)

1. Preheat oven to 350°F. Spray 9-inch round cake pan with nonstick cooking spray.

2. To prepare Cake, in medium bowl, combine flour, baking powder, salt and baking soda.

3. In large bowl, beat granulated sugar and margarine with electric mixer at medium speed until blended. Whisk in apple sauce, ½ cup milk, egg whites and 1 teaspoon vanilla.

4. Add flour mixture to apple sauce mixture; stir until well blended. Pour batter into prepared pan.

5. Bake 35 to 40 minutes or until toothpick inserted in center comes out clean. Cool completely on wire rack. Split cake horizontally in half to make 2 layers.

6. To prepare Filling, prepare pudding mix according to package directions using 1½ cups skim milk. (Or, substitute 1½ cups prepared fat-free vanilla pudding for Filling.)

7. To prepare Chocolate Glaze, in small bowl, sift together powdered sugar and cocoa. Stir in 1 tablespoon milk and ½ teaspoon vanilla. Add water, 1 teaspoon at a time, until of desired spreading consistency. Place one cake layer on serving plate. Spread filling over cake. Top with second cake layer. Spread top of cake with Chocolate Glaze. Let stand until set. Garnish with lemon peel, if desired. Cut into 10 slices. Refrigerate leftovers.   *Makes 10 servings*

Cherry Glazed Chocolate Torte

½ cup (1 stick) butter or margarine,
     melted
1 cup sugar
1 teaspoon vanilla extract
2 eggs
½ cup all-purpose flour
⅓ cup HERSHEY₀S Cocoa
¼ teaspoon baking powder
¼ teaspoon salt
     Cream Layer (recipe follows)
1 can (21 ounces) cherry pie filling,
     divided

Heat oven to 350°F. Grease bottom of 9-inch
springform pan. In large bowl, stir together butter,
sugar and vanilla. Add eggs; using spoon, beat well.
Stir together flour, cocoa, baking powder and salt;
gradually add to egg mixture, beating until well
blended. Spread batter into prepared pan. Bake 25 to
30 minutes or until cake is set. (Cake will be fudgey
and will not test done.) Cool completely in pan on wire
rack. Prepare Cream Layer; spread over top of cake.
Spread 1 cup cherry pie filling over Cream Layer;

refrigerate 3 hours. With knife, loosen cake from side
of pan; remove side of pan. Serve with remaining pie
filling. Garnish as desired. Cover; refrigerate leftover
torte.   *Makes 10 to 12 servings*

Cream Layer

1 **package (8 ounces) cream cheese,
    softened**
1 **cup powdered sugar**
1 **cup frozen non-dairy whipped topping,
    thawed**

In medium bowl, beat cream cheese and powdered
sugar until well blended. Fold in whipped topping.

Almond Chocolate Torte with Raspberry Sauce

2½ cups **BLUE DIAMOND®** Blanched
Whole Almonds, lightly toasted and
divided
9 squares (1 ounce each) semi-sweet
chocolate
¼ cup butter
6 eggs, beaten
¾ cup sugar
2 tablespoons flour
¼ cup brandy
Fudge Glaze (recipe follows)
Raspberry Sauce (recipe follows)

Preheat oven to 350°F. In food processor or blender,
process 1 cup almonds until finely ground. Generously
grease 9-inch round cake pan; sprinkle with
2 tablespoons ground almonds. In top of double
boiler, melt chocolate and butter over simmering
water, blending thoroughly; cool slightly. In large bowl,
beat eggs and sugar. Gradually beat in chocolate
mixture. Add flour, remaining ground almonds and
brandy; mix well. Pour batter into prepared pan.

Bake 25 minutes or until toothpick inserted into
center comes out almost clean. Let cool in pan on wire
rack 10 minutes. Loosen edge; remove from pan. Cool
completely on wire rack.

Prepare Fudge Glaze. Place sheet of waxed paper under wire rack. Pour Fudge Glaze over torte, spreading over top and sides with spatula. Carefully transfer torte to serving plate; let glaze set. Prepare Raspberry Sauce; set aside. Arrange remaining 1½ cups whole almonds, points toward center, in circle around outer edge of torte. Working toward center, repeat circles, overlapping almonds slightly. To serve, pour small amount of Raspberry Sauce on each serving plate; top with slice of torte.   *Makes 10 to 12 servings*

Fudge Glaze: In small saucepan, combine 6 tablespoons water and 3 tablespoons sugar. Simmer over low heat until sugar dissolves. Stir in 3 squares (1 ounce each) semi-sweet chocolate and 1 tablespoon brandy. Heat, stirring occasionally, until chocolate melts and glaze coats back of spoon.

Raspberry Sauce: In blender or food processor, purée 2 packages (10 ounces each) thawed frozen raspberries. Strain raspberry purée through a fine sieve to remove seeds. Stir in sugar to taste.

Mocha Cake Roll with Creamy Chocolate Filling

¾ cup granulated sugar
2 eggs
3 egg whites
¼ cup Prune Purée (page 71) or prepared prune butter
¼ cup coffee-flavored liqueur, divided
2 tablespoons instant coffee granules
1 cup all-purpose flour
¼ cup unsweetened cocoa powder, divided
¼ teaspoon salt
  Powdered sugar
1½ cups low fat nondairy whipped topping
  Additional low fat nondairy whipped topping and chocolate covered coffee beans, for garnish

Preheat oven to 425°F. Coat 13×9×2-inch baking pan with vegetable cooking spray. Line pan with parchment or waxed paper; coat paper with vegetable cooking spray. In top of double boiler or bowl set over simmering water, combine granulated sugar, eggs and egg whites. Beat at high speed with portable electric mixer until tripled in volume, about 5 minutes. Beat in prune purée, 2 tablespoons liqueur and coffee granules until well blended; remove from heat. In medium bowl, combine flour, 2 tablespoons cocoa and salt. Sift flour mixture over egg mixture; gently fold in just until blended. Spread batter evenly in prepared pan. Bake in center of oven 10 minutes or until springy to the touch.

Meanwhile, lay cloth tea towel on work surface; dust evenly with powdered sugar. When cake is done, immediately loosen edges and invert onto towel. Gently peel off paper. Roll cake up in towel from narrow end. Place seam side down on wire rack; cool completely. Gently unroll cooled cake; brush with remaining 2 tablespoons liqueur. Combine whipped topping with remaining 2 tablespoons cocoa. Spread evenly over moistened cake. Reroll cake without towel. Place seam side down on serving plate. Dust with powdered sugar. Garnish with additional whipped topping and coffee beans. Cut into slices.

Makes 12 servings

Favorite recipe from **California Prune Board**

Chocolate Cream-Filled Cake Roll

¾ cup sifted cake flour
¼ cup unsweetened cocoa
½ teaspoon baking powder
¼ teaspoon salt
4 eggs
¾ cup granulated sugar
1 tablespoon water
1 teaspoon vanilla extract
 Powdered sugar
 Cream Filling (recipe follows)
 Chocolate Stars (recipe follows)
 Sweetened whipped cream

1. Preheat oven to 375°F. Grease bottom of 15½×10½×1-inch jelly-roll pan. Line with waxed paper. Grease paper and sides of pan; dust with flour.

2. Combine flour, cocoa, baking powder and salt in small bowl; set aside. Beat eggs in medium bowl with electric mixer on high speed about 5 minutes or until thick and lemon colored. Add granulated sugar, a little at a time, beating well on medium speed; beat until thick and fluffy. Stir in water and vanilla. Fold in flour mixture on low speed until smooth. Spread evenly in prepared pan.

3. Bake 12 to 15 minutes until wooden pick inserted in center comes out clean. Meanwhile, sprinkle towel with powdered sugar. Loosen cake edges and turn out onto prepared towel. Carefully peel off waxed paper. Roll up cake with towel inside, starting with narrow end. Cool, seam side down, 20 minutes on wire rack.

4. Meanwhile, prepare Cream Filling and Chocolate Stars. Unroll cake and spread with Cream Filling. Roll up again, without towel. Cover and refrigerate at least 1 hour before serving. Dust with additional powdered sugar before serving. Place star tip in pastry bag; add sweetened whipped cream. Pipe rosettes on top of cake. Place points of Chocolate Stars into rosettes. Garnish with raspberries and mint, if desired. Store tightly covered in refrigerator.   *Makes 8 to 10 servings*

Cream Filling

- 1 **teaspoon unflavored gelatin**
- ¼ **cup cold water**
- 1 **cup whipping cream**
- 2 **tablespoons powdered sugar**
- 1 **tablespoon orange-flavored liqueur**

Sprinkle gelatin over cold water in small saucepan; let stand 1 minute to soften. Heat over low heat until dissolved, stirring constantly. Cool to room temperature. Beat cream, powdered sugar and liqueur in small chilled bowl with electric mixer on high speed until stiff peaks form. Fold in gelatin mixture on low speed. Cover and refrigerate 5 to 10 minutes.

Chocolate Stars: Melt 2 squares (1 ounce each) semisweet chocolate in heavy small saucepan over low heat, stirring frequently. Pour onto waxed-paper-lined cookie sheet. Spread to ⅛-inch thickness with small metal spatula. Refrigerate about 15 minutes or until firm. Cut out stars with cookie cutter. Carefully lift stars from waxed paper using metal spatula or knife. Refrigerate until ready to use.

Chocolate Angel Food Rolls

CAKE
- 1 package DUNCAN HINES® Angel Food Cake Mix
- 3 tablespoons unsweetened cocoa Confectioners sugar

FILLING
- ½ square (½ ounce) grated semi-sweet chocolate
- 1 container (8 ounces) frozen whipped topping, thawed

DRIZZLE
- 2 squares (2 ounces) semi-sweet chocolate, chopped
- 2 teaspoons CRISCO® all-vegetable shortening

1. Preheat oven to 350°F. Line two 15½×10½×1-inch jelly-roll pans with aluminum foil.

2. For cake, place cake mix, cocoa and water (per package) in large bowl. Prepare cake following package directions. Divide batter into pans. Spread evenly. Cut through batter with knife or spatula to remove large air bubbles. Bake at 350°F for 15 minutes or until set. Invert cakes at once onto lint-free kitchen towels dusted with confectioners sugar. Remove foil carefully. Starting at short end, roll up each cake with towel jelly-roll fashion. Cool completely.

3. For filling, fold grated chocolate into whipped topping. Unroll cakes. Spread half of filling to edges on each cake. Reroll and place seam sides down on serving plate.

4. For drizzle, combine chocolate and shortening in small resealable plastic bag. Place bag in bowl of hot water for several minutes. Dry with paper towel. Knead until blended and chocolate is smooth. Snip pinpoint corner in bag. Drizzle over rolls. Refrigerate until ready to serve.   *Makes 16 to 20 servings*

Quick Chocolate Cupcakes

1½ **cups all-purpose flour**
 ¾ **cup sugar**
 ¼ **cup HERSHEY:S Cocoa**
 1 **teaspoon baking soda**
 ½ **teaspoon salt**
 1 **cup water**
 ¼ **cup vegetable oil**
 1 **tablespoon white vinegar**
 1 **teaspoon vanilla extract**

Heat oven to 375°F. Line muffin cups (2½ inches in diameter) with paper bake cups. In medium bowl, stir together flour, sugar, cocoa, baking soda and salt. Add water, oil, vinegar and vanilla; beat with whisk just until batter is smooth and ingredients are well blended. Fill muffin cups ⅔ full with batter. Bake 16 to 18 minutes or until wooden pick inserted in center comes out clean. Remove from pans to wire rack. Cool completely. Frost as desired.

Makes 1½ dozen cupcakes

🍓 Decadent 🍓

CHEESECAKES

PHILLY 3-STEP™
Pralines and Cream Cheesecake

2 (8-ounce) packages PHILADELPHIA
    BRAND® Cream Cheese, softened
½ cup sugar
½ teaspoon vanilla
2 eggs
½ cup almond brickle chips
1 ready to use graham cracker pie crust
    (6 ounces *or* 9 inch)
3 tablespoons caramel ice cream topping

1. MIX cream cheese, sugar and vanilla at medium speed with electric mixer until well blended. Add eggs; mix until blended. Blend in almond brickle chips.

2. POUR into crust. Dot top of cheesecake batter with topping. Cut through batter with knife several times for marble effect.

3. BAKE at 350°F, 40 minutes or until center is almost set. Cool. Refrigerate 3 hours or overnight.

Makes 8 servings

Chocolate Marble Praline Cheesecake

CRUST

>   1   package DUNCAN HINES® Golden
>   Sugar Cookie Mix
>   1   egg
> ¼   cup CRISCO® Oil or CRISCO®
>   PURITAN® Canola Oil
> 1½ tablespoons water
> ½   cup finely chopped pecans (see Tip)

FILLING

> 1¼ cups firmly packed brown sugar
>   2   tablespoons all-purpose flour
>   3   packages (8 ounces each) cream
>   cheese, softened
>   3   eggs, lightly beaten
> 1½ teaspoons vanilla extract
>   1   square (1 ounce) unsweetened
>   chocolate, melted
> 20 to 25 pecan halves (½ cup)
>   Caramel flavor topping

1. Preheat oven to 350°F.

2. For crust, combine cookie mix, 1 egg, oil, water and chopped pecans in large bowl. Stir until thoroughly blended. Reserve 1 cup dough; set aside (see Note). Press remaining mixture into bottom of ungreased 9-inch springform pan. Bake at 350°F for 22 to 24 minutes or until edge is light brown and center is set. Remove from oven.

3. For filling, combine brown sugar and flour in small bowl; set aside. Place cream cheese in large bowl. Beat at low speed with electric mixer, adding brown sugar mixture gradually. Add beaten eggs and vanilla extract, mixing only until incorporated. Remove 1 cup batter to small bowl; add melted chocolate. Pour remaining plain batter onto warm crust. Drop spoonfuls of chocolate batter over plain batter. Run knife through batters to marble. Arrange pecan halves around top edge. Bake at 350°F for 45 to 55 minutes or until set. Loosen cake from sides of pan with knife or spatula. Cool completely on rack. Refrigerate 2 hours or until ready to serve.

4. To serve, remove sides of pan. Glaze top of cheesecake with caramel flavor topping. Cut into slices and serve with additional caramel flavor topping, if desired. *Makes 12 to 16 servings*

Tip: For added flavor, toast pecans before chopping. Spread pecans in single layer on baking sheet. Toast in 350°F oven for 3 to 5 minutes or until fragrant. Cool completely.

Note: To bake reserved cookie dough, press ¼ cup dough into 3-inch circle on ungreased baking sheet. Repeat with remaining dough. Bake at 375°F for 8 to 10 minutes or until light golden brown. Cool 1 minute on baking sheet. Remove to cooling rack. Makes 4 large cookies.

Butterscotch Cheesecake with Chocolate Drizzle

Graham Cracker Crust (recipe follows)
3 packages (8 ounces each) cream cheese, softened
½ cup sugar
2 tablespoons all-purpose flour
1⅔ cups (10-ounce package) HERSHEY'S Butterscotch Chips
2 tablespoons milk
4 eggs
Chocolate Drizzle (recipe follows)

Prepare Graham Cracker Crust. *Increase oven temperature to 350°F.* In large bowl on medium speed of electric mixer, beat cream cheese, sugar and flour until smooth. In small microwave-safe bowl, place butterscotch chips and milk. Microwave at HIGH (100%) 1 minute; stir. If necessary, microwave at HIGH an additional 15 seconds at a time, stirring after each heating, just until chips are melted when stirred. Blend butterscotch mixture into cream cheese mixture. Add eggs, one at a time, blending well after each addition. Pour mixture over prepared crust. Bake 40 to 45 minutes or until almost set in center. Remove from oven to wire rack. With knife, immediately loosen cake from side of pan. Cool completely; remove side of pan. Prepare Chocolate Drizzle; drizzle over cheesecake. Refrigerate leftover cheesecake.

Makes 12 servings

Graham Cracker Crust

1 cup graham cracker crumbs
3 tablespoons sugar
3 tablespoons butter or margarine,
    melted

Heat oven to 325°F. Stir together crumbs, sugar and butter. Press mixture onto bottom of 9-inch springform pan. Bake 10 minutes. Cool completely.

Chocolate Drizzle

½ cup HERSHEY'S Semi-Sweet
    Chocolate Chips
1 tablespoon shortening (do *not* use
    butter, margarine or oil)

In small microwave-safe bowl, place chocolate chips and shortening. Microwave at HIGH (100%) 30 seconds; stir. If necessary, microwave at HIGH an additional 15 seconds at a time, stirring after each heating, just until chips are melted when stirred.

Triple Layer Cheesecake

Chocolate Crumb Crust (recipe follows)
3 **packages (8 ounces each) cream
   cheese, softened**
¾ **cup sugar**
3 **eggs**
⅓ **cup dairy sour cream**
3 **tablespoons all-purpose flour**
1 **teaspoon vanilla extract**
¼ **teaspoon salt**
1 **cup HERSHEY₀S Butterscotch Chips,
   melted***
1 **cup HERSHEY₀S Semi-Sweet
   Chocolate Chips, melted***
1 **cup HERSHEY₀S Premier White Chips,
   melted***
Triple Drizzle (recipe follows)

*To melt chips, place chips in separate medium microwave-safe
bowls. Microwave at HIGH (100%) 1 minute; stir. If necessary,
microwave at HIGH an additional 15 seconds at a time, stirring after
each heating, just until chips are melted when stirred.

Heat oven to 350°F. Prepare Chocolate Crumb Crust.
In large bowl, beat cream cheese and sugar until
smooth. Add eggs, sour cream, flour, vanilla and salt;
beat until blended. Stir 1⅓ cups batter into melted
butterscotch chips until smooth; pour into prepared
crust. Stir 1⅓ cups batter into melted chocolate chips
until smooth; pour over butterscotch layer. Stir
remaining batter into melted white chips until smooth;
pour over chocolate layer. Bake 55 to 60 minutes or
until almost set in center. Remove from oven to wire

rack. With knife, loosen cake from side of pan. Cool completely; remove side of pan. Prepare Triple Drizzle, if desired; drizzle, one flavor at a time, over top of cheesecake. Refrigerate 3 hours. Cover; refrigerate leftover cheesecake.   *Makes 12 to 14 servings*

Chocolate Crumb Crust

- 1½ **cups vanilla wafer crumbs (45 wafers)**
- ½ **cup powdered sugar**
- ¼ **cup HERSHEY₀S Cocoa**
- ⅓ **cup butter or margarine, melted**

Heat oven to 350°F. Stir together all ingredients. Press mixture onto bottom and 1½ inches up side of 9-inch springform pan. Bake 8 minutes. Cool completely.

Triple Drizzle

- 1 **tablespoon** *each* **HERSHEY₀S Butterscotch Chips, HERSHEY₀S Semi-Sweet Chocolate Chips and HERSHEY₀S Premier White Chips**
- 1½ **teaspoons shortening (do** *not* **use butter, margarine or oil), divided**

Microwave Directions: In small microwave-safe bowl, place butterscotch chips and ½ teaspoon shortening. Microwave at HIGH (100%) 30 seconds; stir. If necessary, microwave on HIGH an additional 15 seconds at a time, stirring after each heating, just until chips are melted when stirred. Repeat procedure with chocolate chips and white chips, using ½ teaspoon shortening for each.

Marble Cheesecake

**HERSHEY:S Chocolate Crumb Crust
(recipe follows)**
3   **packages (8 ounces each) cream
      cheese, softened**
1   **cup sugar, divided**
½   **cup dairy sour cream**
2½ **teaspoons vanilla extract, divided**
3   **tablespoons all-purpose flour**
3   **eggs**
¼   **cup HERSHEY:S Cocoa**
1   **tablespoon vegetable oil**

Prepare HERSHEY®S Chocolate Crumb Crust. *Increase oven temperature to 450°F.* In large bowl on medium speed of electric mixer, beat cream cheese, ¾ cup sugar, sour cream and 2 teaspoons vanilla until smooth. Gradually add flour, beating well. Add eggs, one at a time, beating well after each addition. In medium bowl, stir together cocoa and remaining ¼ cup sugar. Add oil, remaining ½ teaspoon vanilla and 1½ cups cream cheese mixture; blend well. Spoon plain and chocolate batters alternately into prepared crust, ending with spoonfuls of chocolate batter; gently swirl with knife for marbled effect. Bake 10 minutes. *Without opening door, reduce oven temperature to 250°F;* continue baking 30 minutes. Turn off oven; without opening door, leave cheesecake in oven 30 minutes. Remove

from oven to wire rack. With knife, immediately loosen
cheesecake from side of pan; cool completely.
Refrigerate several hours or overnight; remove side of
pan. Cover; refrigerate leftover cheesecake.

Makes 10 to 12 servings

HERSHEY'S Chocolate Crumb Crust

1¼ cups vanilla wafer crumbs (about
    40 wafers)
⅓ cup powdered sugar
⅓ cup HERSHEY'S Cocoa
¼ cup (½ stick) butter or margarine,
    melted

Heat oven to 350°F. In medium bowl, stir together
crumbs, powdered sugar and cocoa; blend in butter.
Press mixture onto bottom and ½ inch up side of
9-inch springform pan. Bake 8 minutes; cool
completely.

Grand Finale Cheesecake

Almond Graham Crust (recipe follows)
1 HERSHEY'S SYMPHONY® Milk
   Chocolate Bar or Milk Chocolate Bar
   With Almonds & Toffee Chips
   (7 ounces), broken into pieces
4 packages (3 ounces each) cream
   cheese, softened
½ cup sugar
2 tablespoons HERSHEY'S Cocoa
⅛ teaspoon salt
2 eggs
1 teaspoon vanilla extract
   Whipped cream (optional)

Prepare Almond Graham Crust. Heat oven to 325°F. In
small microwave-safe bowl, place chocolate. Microwave
at HIGH (100%) 1 minute or until chocolate is melted
and smooth when stirred. In large bowl, beat cream
cheese until smooth. Stir together sugar, cocoa and
salt; blend into cream cheese mixture. Add eggs and
vanilla; beat until well blended. Pour into prepared
crust. Bake 35 to 40 minutes or until set in center.
Remove from oven to wire rack. With knife,
immediately loosen cake from side of pan. Cool
completely; remove side of pan. Refrigerate several
hours before serving. Garnish with whipped cream, if
desired. Cover; refrigerate leftover cheesecake.

Makes 8 servings

Almond Graham Crust

- ¾ **cup graham cracker crumbs**
- ⅔ **cup finely chopped slivered almonds**
- 2 **tablespoons sugar**
- ¼ **cup (½ stick) butter or margarine, melted**

In medium bowl, stir together crumbs, almonds and sugar. Stir in butter. Press mixture onto bottom and up side of 8-inch springform pan.

PHILLY 3-STEP™
Toffee Crunch Cheesecake

- 2 **(8-ounce) packages PHILADELPHIA BRAND® Cream Cheese, softened**
- ½ **cup sugar**
- ½ **teaspoon vanilla**
- 2 **eggs**
- 1 **ready to use graham cracker pie crust (6 ounces *or* 9 inch)**
- 4 **(1.4-ounce) bars chocolate covered English toffee, chopped (1 cup)**

1. MIX cream cheese, sugar and vanilla at medium speed with electric mixer until well blended. Add eggs; mix until blended.

2. POUR into crust. Sprinkle with toffee.

3. BAKE at 350°F, 40 minutes or until center is almost set. Cool. Refrigerate 3 hours or overnight.

Makes 8 servings

Luscious Chocolate Cheesecake

2 **cups (1 pound) nonfat cottage cheese**
¾ **cup liquid egg substitute**
⅔ **cup sugar**
4 **ounces (½ of 8-ounce package)**
   Neufchâtel cheese, softened
⅓ **cup HERSHEY₀S Cocoa or**
   HERSHEY₀S European Style Cocoa
½ **teaspoon vanilla extract**
   Yogurt Topping (recipe follows)
   Sliced strawberries or mandarin orange
   segments (optional)

Heat oven to 300°F. Spray 9-inch springform pan with vegetable cooking spray. In food processor, place cottage cheese, egg substitute, sugar, Neufchâtel cheese, cocoa and vanilla; process until smooth. Pour into prepared pan. Bake 35 minutes or until edges are set. Meanwhile, prepare Yogurt Topping. Carefully spread topping over cheesecake. Continue baking 5 minutes. Remove from oven to wire rack. With knife, loosen cheesecake from side of pan. Cool completely. Cover; refrigerate until chilled. Remove side of pan. Serve with strawberries, if desired. Refrigerate leftover cheesecake.   *Makes 9 servings*

Yogurt Topping

⅔ **cup plain nonfat yogurt**
2 **tablespoons sugar**

In small bowl, stir together yogurt and sugar until well blended.

Chocolate Cheesecake

1½ cups crumbled chocolate wafers
(28 wafers)
6 tablespoons butter, melted
⅔ cup sugar, divided
2 envelopes unflavored gelatin
2 cups milk
2 eggs, separated*
12 ounces semisweet chocolate, broken
2 cups cream-style cottage cheese
1 cup whipping cream, whipped

*Use clean, uncracked eggs.

In small bowl, stir together crumbled wafers and
butter. Press mixture evenly onto bottom and 1½
inches up side of buttered 9-inch springform pan.

In large saucepan, combine ⅓ cup sugar and gelatin.
Stir in milk and egg yolks. Cook and stir over medium
heat until thickened. Stir in chocolate until melted.
Cover and refrigerate until partially set.

In blender, process cottage cheese until smooth; fold
into chilled chocolate mixture. In medium bowl, beat
egg whites with electric mixer on high speed until soft
peaks form. Gradually add remaining ⅓ cup sugar,
beating until stiff peaks form. Gently fold beaten egg
whites into chocolate mixture. Fold in whipped cream.
Pour mixture into prepared pan. Chill at least 4 hours
or until firm. If desired, garnish with whipped cream
and strawberries. *Makes 12 to 16 servings*

Favorite recipe from **Wisconsin Milk Marketing Board**

Bavarian Forest Cheesecake

WHOPPERS® CRUST
  1 package (7 ounces) or 2 cups
     WHOPPERS® Malted Milk Candy,
     crushed
  ½ cup graham cracker crumbs
  ¼ cup butter or margarine, melted

FILLING
  3 packages (8 ounces each) cream
     cheese, softened
  ½ cup sugar
  1 teaspoon vanilla
  6 eggs
  1 package (7 ounces) or 2 cups
     WHOPPERS® Malted Milk Candy,
     crushed

For WHOPPERS® Crust, in small bowl, combine all crust ingredients; mix well. Grease bottom of 9-inch springform pan. Press crust mixture onto bottom of pan. For Filling, preheat oven to 350°F. In large bowl, beat cream cheese until fluffy. Gradually add sugar, beating constantly; beat in vanilla. Add eggs, 1 at a time, beating thoroughly after each addition. Pour batter onto prepared crust.

Bake 30 minutes. Remove from oven; sprinkle 1 package crushed WHOPPERS® over top. Continue baking 10 minutes or until set. Loosen cake from rim of pan; cool completely in pan on wire rack. Cover; refrigerate at least 2 hours. Before serving, remove side of springform pan. Garnish cake with whipped cream, WHOPPERS® and maraschino cherries. Store, covered, in refrigerator.   *Makes 10 to 12 servings*

PHILLY 3-STEP™ Black Forest Cherry Cheesecake

- 2 packages (8 ounces each) PHILADELPHIA BRAND® Cream Cheese, softened
- ½ cup sugar
- ½ teaspoon vanilla
- 2 eggs
- 4 squares BAKER'S® Semi-Sweet Chocolate, melted, slightly cooled
- 1 ready to use chocolate flavored pie crust (6 ounces *or* 9 inch)
- 1 cup thawed COOL WHIP® Whipped Topping
- 1½ cups cherry pie filling
- 1 to 2 tablespoons cherry-flavored liqueur

1. MIX cream cheese, sugar and vanilla with electric mixer on medium speed until well blended. Add eggs; mix until blended. Blend in melted chocolate.

2. POUR into crust.

3. BAKE at 350°F for 40 minutes or until center is almost set. Cool. Refrigerate 3 hours or overnight. Top chilled cheesecake with whipped topping. Mix pie filling and liqueur; spoon over whipped topping. Garnish, if desired.   *Makes 8 servings*

German Chocolate Cheesecake

Coconut-Pecan Graham Crust (recipe
   follows)
4 bars (1 ounce each) HERSHEY'S
   Semi-Sweet Baking Chocolate,
   broken into pieces
3 packages (8 ounces each) cream
   cheese, softened
¾ cup sugar
½ cup dairy sour cream
2 teaspoons vanilla extract
2 tablespoons all-purpose flour
3 eggs
   Coconut-Pecan Topping (recipe follows)

Prepare Coconut-Pecan Graham Crust. Heat oven to
450°F. In small microwave-safe bowl, place chocolate.
Microwave at HIGH (100%) 1 to 1½ minutes or until
chocolate is melted and smooth when stirred. In large
bowl on medium speed of electric mixer, beat cream
cheese, sugar, sour cream and vanilla until smooth.
Add flour; blend well. Add eggs and melted chocolate;
beat until blended. Pour into prepared crust. Bake 10
minutes. *Without opening oven door, reduce oven
temperature to 250°F.* Continue baking 35 minutes.
Remove from oven to wire rack. With knife, loosen
cake from side of pan. Cool completely; remove side of
pan. Prepare Coconut-Pecan Topping; spread over
cheesecake. Refrigerate several hours. Garnish as
desired. Cover; refrigerate leftover cheesecake.

Makes 10 to 12 servings

Coconut-Pecan Graham Crust

1 **cup graham cracker crumbs**
2 **tablespoons sugar**
⅓ **cup butter or margarine, melted**
¼ **cup MOUNDS® Sweetened Coconut
    Flakes**
¼ **cup chopped pecans**

Heat oven to 350°F. In small bowl, combine graham
cracker crumbs and sugar. Stir in butter, coconut and
pecans. Press mixture onto bottom and ½ inch up side
of 9-inch springform pan. Bake 8 to 10 minutes or
until lightly browned. Cool completely.

Coconut-Pecan Topping

½ **cup (1 stick) butter or margarine**
¼ **cup packed light brown sugar**
2 **tablespoons light cream**
2 **tablespoons light corn syrup**
1 **cup MOUNDS® Sweetened Coconut
    Flakes**
½ **cup chopped pecans**
1 **teaspoon vanilla extract**

In small saucepan, melt butter; add brown sugar, light
cream and corn syrup. Cook over medium heat,
stirring constantly, until smooth and bubbly. Remove
from heat. Stir in coconut, pecans and vanilla. Cool
slightly.

PHILLY 3-STEP™ Chocolate Chip Cheesecake

2 (8-ounce) packages PHILADELPHIA
      BRAND® Cream Cheese, softened
½ cup sugar
½ teaspoon vanilla
2 eggs
¾ cup mini semi-sweet chocolate chips,
      divided
1 ready to use graham cracker or
      chocolate flavored pie crust
      (6 ounces *or* 9 inch)

1. MIX cream cheese, sugar and vanilla at medium
speed with electric mixer until well blended. Add eggs;
mix until blended. Stir in ½ cup of the chips.

2. POUR into crust. Sprinkle with remaining ¼ cup
chips.

3. BAKE at 350°F, 40 minutes or until center is almost
set. Cool. Refrigerate 3 hours or overnight.

Makes 8 servings

Peanut Butter Chocolate Chip Cheesecake: Beat ⅓ cup
peanut butter in with cream cheese.

Banana Chocolate Chip Cheesecake: Beat ½ cup
mashed ripe banana in with cream cheese.

OREO® Cheesecake

1 (20-ounce) package OREO® Chocolate
    Sandwich Cookies
⅓ cup margarine, melted
3 (8-ounce) packages cream cheese,
    softened
¾ cup sugar
4 eggs, at room temperature
1 cup dairy sour cream
1 teaspoon vanilla extract
    Whipped cream, for garnish

Preheat oven to 350°F. Finely roll 30 cookies; coarsely
chop 20 cookies. In bowl, combine finely rolled cookie
crumbs and margarine. Press onto bottom and 2
inches up side of 9-inch springform pan; set aside.

In bowl, with electric mixer at medium speed, beat
cream cheese and sugar until creamy. Blend in eggs,
sour cream and vanilla; fold in chopped cookies.
Spread mixture into prepared crust. Bake at 350°F for
60 minutes or until set.

Cool on wire rack at room temperature. Chill at least 4
hours. Halve remaining cookies; remove side of pan. To
serve, garnish with whipped cream and cookie halves.

Makes 12 servings

KAHLÚA® Fantasy Chocolate Cheesecake

Chocolate Crumb Crust (recipe follows)
1½ cups semi-sweet chocolate chips
¼ cup KAHLÚA®
2 tablespoons butter or margarine
2 eggs, beaten
⅓ cup sugar
¼ teaspoon salt
1 cup dairy sour cream
2 packages (8 ounces each) cream
    cheese, softened

Prepare Chocolate Crumb Crust. Place chocolate, KAHLÚA® and butter in heavy, small saucepan. Heat over medium heat until chocolate melts; stir until smooth. Set aside.

Preheat oven to 350°F. Combine eggs, sugar and salt in large bowl. Add sour cream; blend well. Add cream cheese; beat until smooth. Gradually blend in chocolate mixture. Pour into prepared crust. Bake 40 minutes or until filling is barely set in center. With knife, loosen cake from side of pan. Let stand on wire rack 1 hour at room temperature; remove side of pan. Refrigerate, loosely covered, several hours or overnight. Garnish as desired.

Makes 12 to 14 servings

Chocolate Crumb Crust: Combine 1⅓ cups chocolate wafer crumbs, ¼ cup softened butter or margarine and 1 tablespoon sugar in medium bowl. Press firmly in bottom of 9-inch springform pan.

Cappuccino Cheesecake

1 **cup chocolate wafer cookie crumbs**
3 **tablespoons sugar**
3 **tablespoons butter or margarine,**
   melted
4 **packages (8 ounces each)**
   PHILADELPHIA BRAND® Cream
   Cheese, softened
1 **cup sugar**
2 **tablespoons flour**
2 **teaspoons vanilla**
4 **eggs**
1 **tablespoon MAXWELL HOUSE® Instant**
   Coffee
3 **tablespoons coffee-flavored liqueur**

MIX crumbs, 3 tablespoons sugar and butter; press onto bottom and 2 inches up sides of 9-inch springform pan. Bake at 325°F for 10 minutes.

MIX cream cheese, 1 cup sugar, flour and vanilla with electric mixer on medium speed until well blended. Add eggs, 1 at a time, mixing on low speed after each addition, just until blended. Stir instant coffee into liqueur until dissolved. Blend into batter. Pour into crust.

BAKE at 325°F for 55 minutes to 1 hour or until center is almost set. Run knife or metal spatula around rim of pan to loosen cake; cool before removing rim of pan. Refrigerate 4 hours or overnight. Garnish with chocolate-dipped almonds or chocolate-covered coffee beans.   *Makes 12 servings*

PHILLY 3-STEP™ White Chocolate Almond Cheesecake

2 packages (8 ounces each)
   PHILADELPHIA BRAND® Cream
   Cheese, softened
½ cup sugar
½ teaspoon vanilla
2 eggs
1 package (6 ounces) BAKER'S®
   Premium White Chocolate Baking
   Squares, chopped, divided
1 ready to use graham cracker pie crust
   (6 ounces *or* 9 inch)
½ cup chopped almonds

1. MIX cream cheese, sugar and vanilla with electric mixer on medium speed until well blended. Add eggs; mix until blended. Stir in ½ cup of the white chocolate.

2. POUR into crust. Sprinkle with almonds and remaining white chocolate.

3. BAKE at 350°F for 40 minutes or until center is almost set. Cool. Refrigerate 3 hours or overnight. Garnish, if desired.   *Makes 8 servings*

Frozen Chocolate Cheesecake

1½ cups chocolate or vanilla wafer cookie
    crumbs
⅓ cup margarine or butter, melted
10 ounces (1¼ packages) cream cheese,
    softened
½ cup sugar
1 cup (6 ounces) semisweet chocolate
    chips, melted
1 teaspoon vanilla extract
1⅓ cups thawed nondairy whipped topping
¾ cup chopped pecans
    Chocolate curls (optional)

1. Preheat oven to 325°F.

2. Combine cookie crumbs and margarine in small
bowl; press onto bottom and side of 9-inch pie plate.
Bake 10 minutes. Cool crust completely in pan on wire
rack.

3. Combine cream cheese and sugar in large bowl.
Gradually stir melted chocolate chips and vanilla
into cheese mixture. Gently fold whipped topping into
cheese mixture; fold in pecans. Pour cheese filling into
prepared crust and freeze until firm. Garnish with
chocolate curls, if desired.   *Makes 8 servings*

Lemon Cheesecake with Raspberry Sauce

CRUST
- 1 **package DUNCAN HINES® Moist Deluxe Supreme Lemon Cake Mix**
- ½ **cup CRISCO® Oil or CRISCO® PURITAN® Canola Oil**
- ⅓ **cup finely chopped pecans**

FILLING
- 3 **packages (8 ounces each) cream cheese, softened**
- ¾ **cup sugar**
- 2 **tablespoons lemon juice**
- 1 **teaspoon grated lemon peel**
- 3 **eggs, lightly beaten**

SAUCE
- 1 **package (12 ounces) frozen dry pack red raspberries, thawed**
- ⅓ **cup sugar**
  Raspberries, for garnish
  Lemon slices, for garnish
  Mint leaves, for garnish

1. Preheat oven to 350°F. Grease 10-inch springform pan.

2. For crust, combine cake mix and oil in large bowl. Mix well. Stir in pecans. Press mixture into bottom of pan. Bake at 350°F for about 20 minutes or until light golden brown. Remove from oven. *Increase oven temperature to 450°F.*

3. For filling, place cream cheese in large bowl. Beat on low speed with electric mixer, adding ¾ cup sugar gradually. Add lemon juice and lemon peel. Add eggs, mixing only until incorporated. Pour filling onto crust. Bake at 450°F for 5 to 7 minutes. *Reduce oven temperature to 250°F.* Bake 30 minutes longer or until set. Loosen cake from edge of pan with knife or spatula. Cool completely on cooling rack. Refrigerate 2 hours or until ready to serve.

4. For sauce, combine thawed raspberries and ⅓ cup sugar in small saucepan. Bring to boil. Simmer until berries are soft. Strain through sieve into small bowl to remove seeds. Cool completely.

5. To serve, garnish cheesecake with raspberries, lemon slices and mint leaves. Cut into slices and serve with raspberry sauce.   *Makes 12 to 16 servings*

Tip: Overbeating cheesecake batter can incorporate too much air, which may cause the cheesecake to crack during baking.

Chocolate Cherry Cheesecake

CRUST

  1 package (19.8 ounces) DUNCAN
     HINES® Chewy Fudge Brownie Mix,
     divided
  2 tablespoons butter or margarine,
     softened
  1 teaspoon water

FILLING

  3 packages (8 ounces each) cream
     cheese, softened
  ¾ cup sugar
  2 tablespoons all-purpose flour
  3 eggs, lightly beaten
  2 tablespoons lemon juice
  1 teaspoon vanilla extract
  1 can (21 ounces) cherry pie filling

1. Reserve 2½ cups dry brownie mix for Brownies (see recipe).

2. Preheat oven to 350°F. **For crust,** place remaining brownie mix in medium bowl. Cut in butter with pastry blender or 2 knives until mixture is crumbly. Stir in water. Pat mixture into bottom of ungreased 9-inch springform pan. Bake at 350°F for 10 to 12 minutes or until set. Remove from oven. *Increase oven temperature to 450°F.*

3. For filling, place cream cheese in large bowl. Beat at low speed with electric mixer, adding sugar and flour gradually. Add eggs, lemon juice and vanilla extract, mixing only until incorporated. Pour cream cheese filling onto crust. Bake at 450°F for 10 minutes. *Reduce oven temperature to 250°F.* Bake for 28 to 33 minutes longer or until cheesecake is set. Loosen cake from edge of pan with knife or spatula. Cool completely. Remove sides of pan. Spoon cherry pie filling over top. Refrigerate 2 hours. Allow cheesecake to stand at room temperature 15 minutes before serving.   *Makes 12 to 16 servings*

Brownies

2½ **cups reserved brownie mix**
1 **egg**
¼ **cup CRISCO® Oil or CRISCO® PURITAN® Canola Oil**
3 **tablespoons water**

Preheat oven to 350°F. Grease bottom of 8-inch square pan. Combine 2½ cups reserved brownie mix, egg, oil and water in medium bowl. Stir with spoon until well blended, about 50 strokes. Spread in pan. Bake at 350°F for about 25 minutes or until set. Cool completely. Cut into bars.

Makes 9 to 12 brownies

Tip: Make cheesecake for guests and brownies for your children.

Sour Cherry Cheesecake with Macadamia Nut Crust

Macadamia Nut Crust (recipe follows)
1 can (16 ounces) tart red pitted cherries
3 packages (8 ounces each) cream cheese, softened
1 cup sugar
3 eggs
1 teaspoon vanilla extract
1⅔ cups (10-ounce package) HERSHEY'S Premier White Chips
Sour Cherry Sauce (recipe follows)

Heat oven to 350°F. Prepare Macadamia Nut Crust. Drain cherries, reserving juice for sauce. Chop cherries; drain. In large bowl, beat cream cheese until smooth. Add sugar, eggs and vanilla; beat until blended. In medium microwave-safe bowl, place white chips. Microwave at HIGH (100%) 1 minute; stir. If necessary, microwave at HIGH an additional 15 seconds at a time, just until chips are melted when stirred. Blend into cream cheese mixture. Stir in chopped cherries. Pour over prepared crust. Bake 50 to 55 minutes or until almost set in center. Remove from oven to wire rack. With knife, loosen cake from side of pan. Cool completely; remove side of pan. Refrigerate about 3 hours. Prepare Sour Cherry Sauce; spoon over cheesecake. Garnish as desired. Cover; refrigerate leftover cheesecake.   *Makes 10 to 12 servings*

Macadamia Nut Crust

1   **jar (3½ ounces) macadamia nuts, very finely chopped**
¾   **cup graham cracker crumbs**
2   **tablespoons sugar**
¼   **cup (½ stick) butter or margarine, melted**

In medium bowl, combine all ingredients. Press mixture onto bottom of 9-inch springform pan. Bake at 350°F for 8 minutes. Cool.

Sour Cherry Sauce

1   **tablespoon cornstarch**
2   **tablespoons cherry brandy *or* ½ teaspoon almond extract**

In medium saucepan, combine cornstarch and reserved cherry juice (from cheesecake). Cook and stir over medium heat until mixture comes to a boil. Remove from heat; stir in brandy. Cool.

Heavenly Cheesecake

½ cup graham cracker crumbs
4 (8-ounce) packages PHILADELPHIA BRAND® Neufchatel Cheese, ⅓ Less Fat Than Cream Cheese *or* PHILADELPHIA BRAND® FREE® Fat Free Cream Cheese, softened
1 cup sugar
¼ teaspoon almond extract *or* 1 teaspoon vanilla
2 eggs
3 egg whites

• Heat oven to 325°F.

• Lightly grease bottom of 9-inch springform pan. Sprinkle with crumbs.

• Beat Neufchatel cheese, sugar and extract at medium speed with electric mixer until well blended. Add eggs and egg whites, 1 at a time, mixing at low speed after each addition, just until blended. Pour into pan.

• Bake 45 to 50 minutes or until center is almost set. Run knife or metal spatula around rim of pan to loosen cake; cool before removing rim of pan. Refrigerate 4 hours or overnight.

• Garnish with raspberries, strawberries or blueberries and mint leaves.   *Makes 12 servings*

PHILLY 3-STEP™ Blueberry Cheesecake

2   (8-ounce) packages PHILADELPHIA
       BRAND® Cream Cheese, softened
½   cup sugar
½   teaspoon vanilla
2   eggs
1   cup blueberries, divided
1   ready to use graham cracker pie crust
       (6 ounces *or* 9 inch)

1. MIX cream cheese, sugar and vanilla at medium speed with electric mixer until well blended. Add eggs; mix until blended. Stir in ½ cup of the blueberries.

2. POUR into crust. Sprinkle with remaining ½ cup blueberries.

3. BAKE at 350°F, 40 minutes or until center is almost set. Cool. Refrigerate 3 hours or overnight. Garnish with COOL WHIP® Whipped Topping and blueberries.

Makes 8 servings

Individual Microwave Cheesecakes

 Graham Cracker Crust (recipe follows)
1 egg
⅓ cup KARO® Light Corn Syrup
2 tablespoons sugar
1 tablespoon ARGO® or KINGSFORD'S®
 Corn Starch
1 tablespoon lemon juice
1 package (8 ounces) cream cheese, cut
 in cubes
 Fruit, preserves, pie filling or chocolate
 curls

1. Prepare Graham Cracker Crust. Press 1 tablespoon crust mixture into the bottoms of 4 (6-ounce) microwavable custard cups or ramekins. Arrange in circle in microwave oven.

2. Microwave on HIGH (100%), 1 minute, turning once; let stand while preparing filling.

3. In blender or food processor process egg, corn syrup, sugar, corn starch and lemon juice until combined. Gradually add cream cheese; process 1 minute or until completely smooth. Pour into prepared cups. Arrange in circle in microwave oven.

4. Microwave on MEDIUM (50%), 7 to 7½ minutes or just until set, rotating and rearranging three times. Cover and refrigerate 1 hour.

5. Top with fruit, preserves, pie filling or chocolate curls. *Makes 4 servings*

Graham Cracker Crust: In small microwavable bowl microwave 1 tablespoon MAZOLA® Margarine or butter on HIGH (100%), 1 minute or until melted. Stir in ¼ cup graham cracker crumbs and 1 teaspoon sugar until evenly moistened.

Fat-Free Cheesecake

    1   tablespoon NABISCO® Graham Cracker
        Crumbs
 1½   cups nonfat cottage cheese
    1   cup EGG BEATERS® Healthy Real Egg
        Product, divided
   ½   cup sugar
   ½   cup nonfat cream cheese
   ¼   teaspoon grated lemon peel
    1   tablespoon lemon juice

Sprinkle graham cracker crumbs on bottom and up sides of lightly greased 9-inch square baking pan; set aside.

In electric blender container or food processor, blend cottage cheese and ½ cup EGG BEATERS® until smooth, scraping down sides of container as necessary.

In large bowl, with electric mixer at low speed, beat cottage cheese mixture, remaining EGG BEATERS®, sugar, cream cheese, lemon peel and lemon juice for 2 minutes. Pour into prepared pan. Bake at 325°F for 50 minutes or until set and lightly browned. Cool in pan on wire rack. Cover; chill at least 2 hours. To serve, cut into 9 (3-inch) squares.   *Makes 9 servings*

Teddy Drum Cheesecake

2 (11-ounce) packages ROYAL® No-Bake
  Cheesecake
⅓ cup sugar
2 tablespoons cocoa
½ cup margarine, melted
3 cups cold milk
1¾ cups TEDDY GRAHAMS® Graham
  Snacks, any flavor, divided
1 tablespoon colored sprinkles
  Black shoe string licorice, for garnish
2 plastic drinking straws, for garnish
2 large gum drops, for garnish

Mix contents of graham cracker crumb packets, sugar
and cocoa; stir in margarine. Reserve ½ cup crumb
mixture; press remaining crumb mixture onto bottom
of 8- or 9-inch springform pan.

In large bowl, with mixer at low speed, blend milk and
contents of cheesecake filling packets. Beat at medium
speed 3 minutes, scraping bowl occasionally. Fold in
1½ cups graham snacks; spread into prepared pan.
Sprinkle reserved crumbs and colored sprinkles around
cake edge. Chill 3 to 4 hours.

To serve, remove side of pan. Decorate side of
cheesecake with licorice and remaining graham snacks
to resemble drum. Insert a straw in each gum drop;
place on top of cake to resemble drumsticks.

Makes 12 servings

Apple Cheesecake

1 cup graham cracker crumbs
1 cup sugar, divided
1 teaspoon ground cinnamon, divided
3 tablespoons margarine or butter, melted
2 packages (8 ounces each) cream cheese, softened
2 eggs
½ teaspoon vanilla extract
4 cups peeled, thin apple slices (about 2½ pounds apples)
½ cup chopped pecans

1. Preheat oven to 350°F. Combine crumbs, 3 tablespoons sugar, ½ teaspoon cinnamon and margarine in small bowl; mix well. Press crumb mixture onto bottom and side of 9-inch pie plate; bake 10 minutes.

2. Beat cream cheese and ½ cup sugar in large bowl with electric mixer at medium speed until well blended. Add eggs, one at a time, beating well after each addition. Add vanilla; beat until blended. Pour into crust.

3. Combine remaining sugar (about ⅓ cup) and remaining ½ teaspoon cinnamon in large bowl. Add apples; toss gently to coat. Spoon apple mixture over cream cheese mixture; sprinkle top with pecans.

4. Bake 1 hour and 10 minutes or until set. Cool cheesecake completely in pie plate on wire rack; refrigerate. *Makes 8 servings*

Creamy Banana Cheesecake

20   vanilla sandwich cream cookies
¼   cup margarine or butter, melted
3   packages (8 ounces each) cream
     cheese, softened
⅔   cup sugar
2   tablespoons cornstarch
3   eggs
¾   cup mashed bananas (about 2)
½   cup whipping cream
2   teaspoons vanilla extract
¼   fresh peeled pineapple, cut in chunks *or*
     1 can (20 ounces) pineapple chunks,
     drained
1   pint strawberries, cut into halves
2   tablespoons hot fudge ice cream
     topping
    Mint leaves (optional)

1. Preheat oven to 350°F. Place cookies in food processor or blender; process with on/off pulses until finely crushed. Add margarine; process with pulses until blended. Press crumb mixture onto bottom of 10-inch springform pan; refrigerate.

2. Beat cream cheese in large bowl with electric mixer at medium speed until creamy. Add sugar and cornstarch; beat until blended. Add eggs, one at a time, beating well after each addition. Beat in bananas, whipping cream and vanilla.

3. Pour cream cheese mixture into prepared crust. Place pan on cookie sheet and bake 15 minutes. *Reduce oven temperature to 200°F.* Continue baking 75 minutes or until center is almost set. Loosen edge of cheesecake; cool completely on wire rack before removing rim of pan.

4. Refrigerate cheesecake, uncovered, 6 hours or overnight. Place pineapple and strawberries over top of cake. Allow cheesecake to stand at room temperature 15 minutes before serving. For fudge drizzle, place topping in small resealable plastic freezer bag; seal bag. Microwave at HIGH 20 seconds. Cut off tiny corner of bag; drizzle over fruit. Garnish with mint leaves, if desired. *Makes 8 servings*

🍓 Luscious 🍓

COOL CREATIONS

Ice Cream Cookie Sandwich

2 pints chocolate chip ice cream, softened
1 package DUNCAN HINES® Moist
   Deluxe Dark Chocolate Fudge
   Cake Mix
½ cup butter or margarine, softened

1. Line bottom of one 9-inch round cake pan with aluminum foil. Spread ice cream in pan. Return to freezer until firm. Run knife around edge of pan to loosen ice cream. Remove from pan. Wrap in foil and return to freezer.

2. Preheat oven to 350°F. Line bottom of two 9-inch round cake pans with aluminum foil. Place cake mix in large bowl. Add butter. Mix until crumbs form. Place half the cake mix in each pan. Press lightly. Bake at 350°F for 15 minutes or until browned around edges; do not overbake. Cool 10 minutes. Remove from pans. Remove foil from cookie layers. Cool completely.

3. To assemble, place cookie layer on serving plate. Top with ice cream. Peel off foil. Place second cookie layer on top. Wrap in foil and freeze 2 hours. To keep longer, store in airtight container.

Makes 10 to 12 servings

Tip: You can use lemon sherbet and DUNCAN HINES® Moist Deluxe Lemon Supreme Cake Mix in place of chocolate chip ice cream and Moist Deluxe Dark Chocolate Fudge Cake Mix.

Crunchy Nutty Ice Cream Sundaes

Peanut Butter Sauce (recipe follows)
Coconut Crunch (recipe follows)
1 **pint vanilla ice cream**

Prepare Peanut Butter Sauce and Coconut Crunch.
Scoop ice cream into sundae dishes. Spoon prepared
sauce over ice cream; sprinkle prepared crunch over
top. Serve immediately. *Makes 4 servings*

Peanut Butter Sauce

1 **cup REESE'S® Peanut Butter Chips**
⅓ **cup milk**
¼ **cup whipping cream**
¼ **teaspoon vanilla extract**

In medium saucepan over low heat, heat peanut butter
chips, milk and whipping cream, stirring constantly
until chips are melted. Remove from heat; stir in
vanilla. Cool to room temperature.

Coconut Crunch

½ **cup MOUNDS® Sweetened Coconut**
   Flakes
½ **cup chopped nuts**
1 **tablespoon butter or margarine**

Heat oven to 325°F. In baking pan, combine coconut,
nuts and butter. Toast in oven 6 to 8 minutes or until
mixture is lightly browned, stirring often. (Watch
carefully so mixture does not burn.) Cool completely.

Mocha Parfait

1½   tablespoons margarine
⅓   cup unsweetened cocoa powder
1   cup boiling water
½   cup sugar
1   tablespoon instant coffee granules
1   teaspoon vanilla extract
1   pint coffee-flavored nonfat frozen yogurt
12   whole coffee beans (optional)

1. Melt margarine in heavy saucepan over low heat. Add cocoa; cook and stir 3 minutes. Add boiling water, sugar and coffee; cook and stir until thickened. Remove from heat; stir in vanilla. Cool.

2. Place 2 tablespoons frozen yogurt in bottom of each of 4 parfait glasses. Top each with 1 tablespoon sauce. Top sauce with another 2 tablespoons frozen yogurt; top frozen yogurt with 2 tablespoons sauce. Repeat layering twice more. Top each parfait with 3 coffee beans, if desired.   *Makes 4 servings*

Frozen Brandy Cream in Brandy Lace Cups

4 egg yolks
⅓ cup KARO® Light Corn Syrup
⅓ cup sugar
2 tablespoons brandy*
1 cup heavy or whipping cream
Brandy Lace Cups, prepared
    (recipe follows)

1. In small bowl with mixer at high speed, beat egg yolks until light and fluffy, about 10 minutes.

2. Meanwhile, in 1-quart saucepan combine corn syrup and sugar. Stirring frequently, bring to full boil over medium heat. Without stirring, boil 2 minutes or until temperature on candy thermometer reaches 240°F.

3. Beating constantly, gradually pour hot syrup in a thin, steady stream into egg yolk mixture. Continue beating until thick and completely cool, about 20 minutes. Gently fold in brandy.

4. In chilled mixer bowl beat cream until stiff. Lightly fold about half of brandy mixture into whipped cream. Gently fold in remaining brandy mixture. Cover; freeze 4 to 5 hours or overnight.

5. Just before serving, spoon into Brandy Lace Cups. If desired, garnish each cup with fruit.

Makes about 2½ cups

*Or, use 2 tablespoons orange juice plus ½ teaspoon grated orange peel.

Brandy Lace Cups

¼ cup KARO® Light or Dark Corn Syrup
¼ cup (½ stick) MAZOLA® Margarine or
      butter
¼ cup sugar
½ cup flour
¼ cup very finely chopped pecans or
      walnuts
2 tablespoons brandy
1 ounce semisweet chocolate, melted
      (optional)

1. Preheat oven to 350°F. Grease 2 (15½×12-inch)
cookie sheets.

2. In small saucepan combine corn syrup, margarine
and sugar. Stirring constantly, bring to full boil over
medium heat. Remove from heat. Stir in flour, nuts
and brandy.

3. Drop 4 rounded tablespoonfuls of batter about
7 inches apart onto each prepared cookie sheet.

4. Bake 6 to 8 minutes or until golden. Cool on cookie
sheet 1 minute or until cookies can be lifted from sheet
but are still pliable. Remove cookies with spatula;
drape shiny-side down over bottoms of drinking glasses
or 6-ounce custard cups, pressing gently to form cups.
If cookies harden before shaping, reheat briefly on
cookie sheets.

5. Cool cups completely. Store in airtight container. If
desired, drizzle cups with melted chocolate just before
filling.   *Makes 8 to 10 dessert cups*

Double Almond Ice Cream

3 cups whipping cream
1 cup milk
¾ cup plus 2 tablespoons sugar, divided
4 egg yolks, beaten
1 tablespoon vanilla extract
2 teaspoons almond extract
2 tablespoons butter
1½ cups BLUE DIAMOND® Chopped
Natural Almonds

Combine cream, milk and ¾ cup sugar in medium saucepan. Cook and stir over medium heat until sugar is dissolved and mixture is hot. Gradually add 1 cup cream mixture to beaten egg yolks, whisking constantly. When mixture is smooth, strain into double boiler. Gradually pour in remaining cream mixture, whisking constantly. Cook over simmering water, stirring, until mixture thickens slightly and coats the back of a spoon, about 8 minutes. *Do not boil.* Stir in extracts. Cool.

Meanwhile, melt butter and stir in remaining 2 tablespoons sugar in small saucepan. Cook and stir over medium heat until sugar begins to bubble (about 30 seconds). Add almonds and cook and stir over medium heat until golden and well coated; cool. Stir almonds into ice cream mixture. Pour into ice cream freezer container. Freeze according to manufacturer's instructions.   *Makes 1 quart*

Italian Ice

1 **cup sweet or dry fruity white wine**
1 **cup water**
1 **cup sugar**
1 **cup fresh lemon juice**
2 **egg whites**
  Fresh berries (optional)
  Mint leaves (optional)

1. Place wine and water in small saucepan; add sugar. Cook over medium-high heat until sugar dissolves and syrup boils, stirring frequently. Cover; boil 1 minute. Uncover; adjust heat and simmer 10 minutes without stirring. Remove from heat. Refrigerate 1 hour or until syrup is completely cool.

2. Stir lemon juice into cooled syrup. Pour into 9-inch round cake pan. Freeze 1 hour. Stir mixture with fork, breaking up ice crystals. Freeze 1 hour more or until firm but not solid. Meanwhile, place empty medium bowl in freezer to chill.

3. Beat egg whites in small bowl with electric mixer at high speed until stiff peaks form. Remove lemon ice mixture from cake pan to chilled bowl. Immediately beat ice with whisk or fork until smooth. Fold in egg whites; mix well. Spread egg mixture evenly into same cake pan. Freeze 30 minutes. Immediately stir with fork; cover cake pan with foil. Freeze at least 3 hours or until firm. To serve, scoop Italian Ice into fluted champagne glasses or dessert dishes. Serve with berries and garnish with mint leaves, if desired.

Makes 4 servings

Simple Spumoni

  2 cups whipping cream
  ⅔ cup sweetened condensed milk
  ½ teaspoon rum flavoring
  1 can (21 ounces) cherry pie filling
  ½ cup chopped almonds
  ½ cup miniature chocolate chips

Combine cream, sweetened condensed milk and rum
flavoring in large bowl; refrigerate 30 minutes. Beat
just until soft peaks form. *Do not overbeat.* Fold in
remaining ingredients. Pour into 8×8-inch pan. Cover;
freeze about 4 hours or until firm. Scoop out to serve.
Garnish as desired.   *Makes about 1 quart*

Favorite recipe from **Cherry Marketing Institute, Inc.**

White Chocolate Ice Cream

  1 cup BLUE DIAMOND® Whole Natural
      Almonds, coarsely chopped
  1 tablespoon butter
  3 cups whipping cream
  1 cup milk
  4 egg yolks
  ¾ cup sugar
  1 tablespoon vanilla extract
  ½ cup kirsch
  1 cup grated white chocolate

Sauté almonds in butter in skillet over medium heat
until crisp; reserve. Combine cream and milk in

saucepan; cook over medium heat until skin forms on surface. Beat yolks and sugar with vanilla in medium bowl; gradually add cream mixture, whisking constantly. Strain into double boiler and cook over simmering water, stirring, until mixture thickens and lightly coats the back of a spoon, about 10 minutes. *Do not boil.* Remove from heat; add kirsch and white chocolate, stirring until chocolate melts. Cool to room temperature. Add almonds. Pour into ice cream freezer container. Freeze according to manufacturer's instructions. *Makes 1 quart*

Berry Good Sorbet

- 1 **pint blueberries**
- 1 **package (10 ounces) frozen raspberries in syrup, thawed**
- 1½ **cups ginger ale**
- ¾ **cup KARO® Light Corn Syrup**
- ¼ **cup sugar**
- 2 **tablespoons lemon juice**

1. In blender or food processor purée blueberries and raspberries until smooth. Strain over large bowl, pressing juice and pulp through strainer with rubber spatula. Discard seeds.

2. Stir in ginger ale, corn syrup, sugar and lemon juice.

3. Pour into container of ice cream maker and freeze according to manufacturer's directions.

Makes about 1½ quarts

Citus Sorbet

1 can (12 ounces) frozen DOLE®
    Mandarin Tangerine or Orchard
    Peach Juice Concentrate
1 can (8 ounces) DOLE® Crushed
    Pineapple or Pineapple Tidbits,
    drained
½ cup nonfat or low fat plain yogurt
2½ cups cold water

• **Combine** frozen concentrate, pineapple and yogurt in blender or food processor container; blend until smooth. Stir in water.

• **Pour** mixture into container of ice cream maker.* Freeze according to manufacturer's directions.

• **Serve** sorbet in dessert dishes.

Makes 10 servings

*Or, pour sorbet mixture into 8-inch square, metal pan; cover. Freeze 1½ to 2 hours or until slightly firm. Place in large bowl; beat with electric mixer on medium speed 1 minute or until slushy. Return mixture to metal pan; repeat freezing and beating steps. Freeze until firm, about 6 hours or overnight.

Passion-Banana Sorbet: Substitute DOLE® Pine-Passion-Banana or Pine-Guava-Banana Frozen Juice Concentrate for mandarin tangerine juice concentrate. Prepare sorbet as directed above except reduce water to 2 cups and omit canned pineapple.

Champagne Sorbet

¼ cup sugar
1 envelope unflavored gelatin
½ cup water
2½ cups white champagne
1 cup KARO® Light Corn Syrup
2 tablespoons lemon juice
Raspberry Sauce (recipe follows)
Fresh berries (optional)

1. In 3-quart saucepan mix sugar and gelatin. Stir in water; let stand 1 minute. Stirring constantly, cook over low heat 5 minutes or until gelatin is dissolved; remove from heat. Stir in champagne, corn syrup and lemon juice until smooth.

2. Pour into 8- or 9-inch square baking pan. Cover; freeze until firm.

3. Spoon frozen champagne mixture into chilled large bowl. With mixer at low speed, beat until smooth but not melted. Pour into pan or freezer container. Cover; freeze until firm.

4. Scoop into serving glasses. Top with Raspberry Sauce. If desired, garnish with fresh berries.

Makes 12 servings

Raspberry Sauce: In blender or food processor, purée 1 package (10 ounces) frozen raspberries in syrup, thawed; strain to remove seeds. Stir in ⅓ cup KARO® Light Corn Syrup. *Makes 1¼ cups*

Rapid Raspberry Pie

1 quart vanilla ice cream, softened
1 pint raspberry sherbet, softened
¼ cup raspberry-flavored liqueur*
1 (6-ounce) KEEBLER® READY-CRUST®
   Chocolate Flavored Pie Crust (reserve
   plastic lid)
   Fresh or frozen dry-pack raspberries,
   mint leaves and chocolate curls for
   garnish

In a large bowl, with electric mixer at medium speed, beat ice cream, sherbet and liqueur until well blended.

Spoon mixture into pie crust and smooth top. Cover with reserved plastic lid and freeze at least 1 hour or until firm. (Pie can also be wrapped airtight and frozen for up to 1 month.)

Remove pie from freezer 15 minutes before serving to soften slightly. Garnish with raspberries, mint leaves and chocolate curls.   *Makes 8 servings*

*¼ cup thawed, undiluted raspberry juice concentrate or cranberry-raspberry juice concentrate may be substituted for liqueur.

Iced Coffee and Chocolate Pie

2   envelopes unflavored gelatin
¼   cup cold skim milk
1   cup skim milk, heated to boiling
2   cups vanilla ice milk
⅓   cup sugar
2   tablespoons instant coffee granules
1   teaspoon vanilla extract
1   (6-ounce) KEEBLER® READY-CRUST®
      Chocolate Flavored Pie Crust
      Reduced-calorie whipped topping
      (optional)
      Chocolate curls (optional)

In blender container, sprinkle gelatin over ¼ cup cold milk; mix on low. Let stand 3 to 4 minutes to soften. Add hot milk; cover and mix on low until gelatin dissolves, about 2 minutes. Add ice milk, sugar, coffee granules and vanilla. Cover and mix until smooth. Pour into KEEBLER® READY-CRUST®.

Refrigerate at least 2 hours. Garnish with whipped topping and chocolate curls, if desired.

Makes 1 pie, 8 servings

KAHLÚA® Ice Cream Pie

 1 (9-ounce) package chocolate wafer
   cookies
 ½ cup unsalted butter, melted
 10 tablespoons KAHLÚA®, divided
 1 teaspoon espresso powder
 3 ounces semi-sweet chocolate, chopped
 1 tablespoon unsalted butter
 1 pint vanilla, coffee or chocolate chip ice
   cream
 1 pint chocolate ice cream
 ¾ cup whipping cream, whipped
   Chocolate-covered coffee beans, for
   garnish

In food processor, place about half of cookies, breaking
into pieces. Process to make fine crumbs. Repeat with
remaining cookies. Add ½ cup melted butter and
process with on-off pulses, just to blend. Press crumbs
evenly onto bottom and up side of 9-inch pie plate.
Press crumbs evenly to rim. Bake at 325°F for
10 minutes. Cool completely.

In small saucepan, heat 6 tablespoons KAHLÚA®
and espresso powder over low heat until warmed and
espresso powder has dissolved. Stir in chocolate and
1 tablespoon butter; stir until melted and smooth. Cool
completely.

Transfer vanilla ice cream to electric mixer bowl and
allow to soften slightly. Add 2 tablespoons KAHLÚA®
and beat on low speed to blend. Spread over bottom of

cooled crust and freeze until firm. Spread cooled chocolate mixture over ice cream in pie. Freeze until firm.

Transfer chocolate ice cream to mixer bowl; blend in remaining 2 tablespoons KAHLÚA®. Spread chocolate ice cream over sauce in pie. Freeze until firm.

To serve, pipe decorative border of whipped cream on pie around inside edge. Garnish with chocolate-covered coffee beans. *Makes one 9-inch pie*

Black Magic Pie

       42 OREO® Chocolate Sandwich Cookies
        2 tablespoons margarine, melted
        1 quart chocolate ice cream
        1 pint vanilla ice cream, softened
       ½   cup whipped topping
           Chocolate fudge sauce

Finely crush 22 cookies. Mix 1¼ cups cookie crumbs and margarine; set aside remaining crumbs. Press onto bottom of 9-inch pie plate. Stand 14 cookies around edge of plate, pressing lightly into crust.

Scoop chocolate ice cream into balls; arrange in prepared crust. Coarsely chop remaining 6 cookies; sprinkle over ice cream scoops. Spread softened vanilla ice cream evenly over cookie layer; freeze 15 minutes. Top with a layer of reserved cookie crumbs, pressing gently into ice cream. Freeze several hours or overnight. To serve, garnish with whipped topping and fudge sauce. *Makes 8 servings*

Frozen Butter-Pecan Pie

2 packages (3 ounces each) cream
    cheese, softened
¾ cup KARO® Dark Corn Syrup
⅓ cup packed brown sugar
½ cup milk
1 teaspoon vanilla
1 cup chopped pecans
1 prepared (9-inch) graham cracker crust
1 cup heavy or whipping cream, whipped
    Pecan halves for garnish

1. In large bowl with mixer at high speed, beat cream cheese, corn syrup and brown sugar until smooth. With mixer at medium speed beat in milk and vanilla until blended. Stir in pecans. Pour into crust.

2. Freeze 6 hours or until firm. Garnish with whipped cream and pecan halves. *Makes 8 servings*

HERSHEY'S Cocoa Cream Pie

½ cup HERSHEY'S Cocoa
1¼ cups sugar
⅓ cup cornstarch
¼ teaspoon salt
3 cups milk
3 tablespoons butter or margarine
1½ teaspoons vanilla extract
1 baked 9-inch pie crust or graham
    cracker crumb crust, cooled
    Sweetened whipped cream

In medium saucepan, stir together cocoa, sugar, cornstarch and salt. Gradually add milk, stirring until smooth. Cook over medium heat, stirring constantly, until mixture comes to a boil; boil 1 minute. Remove from heat; stir in butter and vanilla. Pour into prepared crust. Press plastic wrap directly onto surface. Cool to room temperature. Refrigerate 6 to 8 hours. Serve with sweetened whipped cream. Garnish as desired. Cover; refrigerate leftover pie. *Makes 6 to 8 servings*

Frozen Lime Cheesecake Pie

½ **cup milk**
½ **cup sugar**
⅓ **cup KARO® Light Corn Syrup**
2 **teaspoons grated lime peel**
¼ **cup lime juice**
1 **package (8 ounces) cream cheese, cut into cubes**
1 **prepared (9-inch) graham cracker crumb crust**
1 **cup heavy or whipping cream, whipped**
   Additional grated lime peel for garnish

1. In blender container combine milk, sugar, corn syrup, lime peel and juice. Cover and blend on medium speed until smooth. With blender running, gradually add cream cheese cubes; blend just until smooth. Pour into crust.

2. Freeze several hours or overnight. Garnish with whipped cream and grated lime peel.

Makes 8 servings

Chilled Lemon Pie

1   envelope unflavored gelatin
¼   cup lemon juice
2   packages (8 ounces each)
        PHILADELPHIA BRAND® Cream
        Cheese, softened
½   cup sugar
1   container (8 ounces) lemon yogurt
½   teaspoon grated lemon peel
1   cup whipping cream, whipped
1   baked pastry shell (9 inch)
        Currant Raspberry Sauce (recipe
        follows)

SPRINKLE gelatin over juice in small saucepan. Let stand 5 minutes to soften. Cook and stir on low heat until gelatin is completely dissolved. Do not boil.

MIX cream cheese and sugar with electric mixer on medium speed until well blended. Blend in yogurt and peel. Stir in gelatin. Refrigerate until mixture is slightly thickened but not set.

FOLD in whipped cream. Spoon into crust. Refrigerate several hours or overnight until firm. Serve with Currant Raspberry Sauce. Garnish, if desired.

Makes 8 to 10 servings

Currant Raspberry Sauce

1   package (10 ounces) frozen red
        raspberries, thawed
½   cup KRAFT® Red Currant Jelly
4   teaspoons cornstarch

PLACE raspberries and jelly in blender or food processor fitted with steel blade; cover. Process until well blended. Strain.

STIR cornstarch and raspberry mixture in small saucepan until smooth. Bring to boil on medium heat, stirring constantly. Cook until thickened, stirring constantly. Cool.

Frozen Strawberry Cream Cheese Pie

>   1   package (8 ounces) PHILADELPHIA
>   BRAND® FREE® Fat Free Cream
>   Cheese, softened
>   2   tablespoons sugar
>   1   package (10 ounces) frozen
>   strawberries in syrup, thawed
>   1   cup thawed COOL WHIP® LITE®
>   Whipped Topping
>   ¾   cup low-fat granola cereal

BEAT cream cheese with electric mixer on medium speed until smooth. Add sugar and strawberries, mixing until blended. Gently stir in whipped topping.

SPRINKLE granola over bottom of 9-inch pie plate; pour cream cheese mixture over granola. Cover loosely with aluminum foil. Freeze several hours or overnight. Let stand 10 minutes at room temperature before serving. Garnish with COOL WHIP® LITE® Whipped Topping and mint leaves, if desired.

Makes 6 servings

Strawberry Daiquiri Dessert

1 package (3 ounces) ladyfingers, thawed
   if frozen, split in half horizontally
2 tablespoons light rum or apricot nectar
1 container (8 ounces) thawed nondairy
   whipped topping, divided
1 package (8 ounces) cream cheese,
   softened
1 package (16 ounces) frozen
   strawberries, thawed
1 can (10 ounces) frozen strawberry
   daiquiri mix, thawed
   Fresh strawberries (optional)

1. Place ladyfinger halves, cut sides up, in bottom of
11×7-inch dish. Brush with rum.

2. Reserve 1 cup whipped topping in small bowl;
refrigerate, covered.

3. Place cream cheese in food processor; process until
fluffy. Add remaining whipped topping, thawed frozen
strawberries and daiquiri mix; process with on/off
pulses until blended. Pour over ladyfingers.

4. Freeze 6 hours or overnight. Remove from freezer.
Allow dish to stand at room temperature 20 to
30 minutes before serving. Garnish with remaining
whipped topping and fresh strawberries, if desired.
Store any leftover dessert in freezer.

Makes 10 servings

Raspberry Cream Cheese Layered Dessert

1 box (7¾ ounces) reduced-fat chocolate cream-filled cookies, crushed
3 tablespoons reduced-fat tablespread, melted
1 package (8 ounces) PHILADELPHIA BRAND® FREE® Fat Free Cream Cheese, softened
¼ cup sugar
½ cup thawed COOL WHIP® LITE® Whipped Topping
1 cup boiling water
1 package (4-serving size) JELL-O® Brand Raspberry Flavor Gelatin
1 package (10 ounces) frozen red raspberries in light syrup

MIX crumbs and tablespread; press into 8-inch square baking dish. Refrigerate.

BEAT cream cheese with electric mixer on medium speed until smooth. Add sugar, mixing until blended. Gently stir in whipped topping. Pour over crust. Refrigerate.

STIR boiling water into gelatin in medium bowl 2 minutes or until completely dissolved. Stir in fruit until it begins to separate and thaw. Refrigerate until thickened but not set. Spoon over cream cheese layer. Refrigerate until gelatin layer is firm, about 6 hours or overnight.   *Makes 9 servings*

Grasshopper Dessert

CRUST

1 package DUNCAN HINES® Moist
   Deluxe Dark Chocolate Fudge Cake
   Mix, divided

1 egg

½ cup butter or margarine, softened

FILLING

3 cups miniature marshmallows

½ cup milk

⅓ cup green crème de menthe

2 tablespoons white crème de cacao

1½ cups whipping cream, chilled

1. Preheat oven to 350°F. Grease and flour
13×9×2-inch pan. Remove ½ cup cake mix and spread
in 8-inch ungreased baking pan. Toast in oven for
7 minutes. Cool.

2. For crust, combine remaining cake mix, egg and
butter in large bowl. Mix until crumbs form. Press
lightly into prepared 13×9×2-inch pan. Bake at 350°F
for 15 minutes. Cool.

3. For filling, heat marshmallows and milk in medium
saucepan over low heat. Stir constantly until
marshmallows melt. Refrigerate until thickened. Stir
crème de menthe and crème de cacao into
marshmallow mixture.

4. Beat whipping cream until stiff in large bowl. Fold
in marshmallow mixture. Pour onto crust. Dust top
with cooled toasted dry mix. Refrigerate until ready to
serve. Cut into squares. *Makes 12 servings*

Tropical Frozen Mousse

2½ cups mango chunks (2 to 4 mangos,
        peeled and cut into bite-size pieces)
⅓ cup sugar
1 tablespoon kirsch
1 teaspoon fresh lime juice
¼ teaspoon grated lime peel
2 cups whipped cream
    Mango slices and fresh mint leaves for
    garnish

1. Place mango chunks in food processor or blender container. Cover; process until smooth. Blend in sugar, kirsch, lime juice and lime peel. Fold whipped cream into mango mixture. Pour into sherbet glasses.

2. Cover and freeze 4 hours or until firm. Let stand at room temperature 30 minutes before serving. Garnish with mango slices and mint leaves just before serving.

Makes 6 servings

Strawberry Chocolate Roll

3 large eggs, separated
½ cup sugar
5 ounces semisweet chocolate, melted
⅓ cup water
1 teaspoon vanilla extract
¾ cup all-purpose flour
1 teaspoon baking powder
½ teaspoon baking soda
¼ teaspoon salt
Unsweetened cocoa
½ cup seedless strawberry or raspberry
jam
2 pints strawberry ice cream, softened

1. Preheat oven to 350°F. Line 15×10-inch jelly-roll pan with foil, extending foil 1 inch over ends of pan. Grease and flour foil.

2. Beat egg yolks and sugar in medium bowl until light and fluffy. Beat in melted chocolate. Add water and vanilla. Mix until smooth. Sift flour, baking powder, baking soda and salt together. Add to chocolate mixture.

3. Using clean beaters and large bowl, beat egg whites until soft peaks form. Gently fold in chocolate mixture. Pour into prepared pan.

4. Bake 8 to 9 minutes or until wooden pick inserted into center comes out clean. Carefully loosen sides of cake from foil. Invert cake onto towel sprinkled with cocoa. Peel off foil. Starting at short end, roll warm cake, jelly-roll fashion with towel inside. Cool cake completely.

5. Unroll cake and remove towel. Spread cake with jam. Spread ice cream, leaving a ¼-inch border. Roll up cake. Wrap tightly in plastic wrap or foil. Freeze. Allow cake to stand at room temperature 10 minutes before cutting and serving.   *Makes 8 to 12 servings*

Rainbow Sorbet Torte

    4 **pints assorted flavors sorbet**
    1 **package DUNCAN HINES® Moist**
       Deluxe White Cake Mix
       Assorted fruit, for garnish

1. Line bottom of 8-inch round cake pan with aluminum foil. Soften one pint of sorbet. Spread evenly in pan. Freeze until firm. Run knife around edge of pan to loosen sorbet. Remove from pan. Wrap in foil and return to freezer. Repeat for other flavors.

2. Preheat oven to 350°F. Grease and flour two 8-inch round cake pans. Prepare, bake and cool cake following package directions for No Cholesterol recipe.

3. To assemble torte, cut both cake layers in half horizontally. Place one cake layer on serving plate. Top with one layer sorbet. Peel off foil. Repeat layers. Wrap foil around plate and cake. Return to freezer until ready to serve. To serve, garnish top with fruit.
          Makes 10 to 12 servings

Raspberry Tortoni Cake Roll

Raspberry Tortoni Filling
(recipe follows)
3 eggs, separated
¾ cup granulated sugar
¼ cup skim milk
1 teaspoon vanilla extract
¾ cup all-purpose flour
1½ teaspoons baking powder
¼ teaspoon salt
¼ teaspoon cream of tartar
Powdered sugar
¼ cup fresh raspberries (optional)
Mint sprigs (optional)

1. Prepare Raspberry Tortoni Filling. Set aside.

2. Lightly grease 15×10×1-inch jelly-roll pan and line with waxed paper; lightly grease and flour paper. Preheat oven to 400°F. Beat egg yolks in medium bowl with electric mixer at high speed 1 minute; gradually beat in granulated sugar until yolks are thick and lemon colored, about 5 minutes. Beat in milk and vanilla; mix in flour, baking powder and salt.

3. Beat egg whites in medium bowl at high speed until foamy; add cream of tartar and beat until stiff peaks form. Fold about one-third egg white mixture into cake batter; gently fold cake batter into remaining egg white mixture. Spread batter evenly in prepared pan.

4. Bake 8 to 10 minutes or until cake begins to brown. Immediately invert onto clean towel that has been sprinkled with 1 tablespoon powdered sugar. Peel off waxed paper; roll cake up in towel and cool on wire rack only 10 minutes.

5. Gently unroll cake and spread with Raspberry Tortoni Filling. Roll cake up; wrap in plastic wrap or aluminum foil and freeze until firm, at least 8 hours or overnight.

6. Remove cake from freezer; unwrap and trim ends, if uneven. Place cake on serving plate. Sprinkle with additional powdered sugar. Garnish with raspberries and mint, if desired.   *Makes 12 servings*

Raspberry Tortoni Filling

2   **cups fresh or frozen unsweetened raspberries, thawed, drained and divided**
1   **tablespoon granulated sugar**
2   **envelopes (1.3 ounces each) whipped topping mix**
1   **cup 1% low-fat milk**
½   **teaspoon rum or sherry extract (optional)**
¼   **cup pistachio nuts or coarsely chopped blanched almonds**

1. Place 1 cup raspberries in food processor or blender; process until smooth. Strain and discard seeds. Sprinkle sugar over remaining 1 cup raspberries.

2. Beat whipped topping mix with milk in medium bowl at high speed until stiff peaks form; fold in raspberry purée and rum, if desired. Fold in sugared raspberries and nuts.   *Makes 4 cups*

Chocolate Tortoni

8   squares (1 ounce each) semisweet
      chocolate
⅔   cup KARO® Light or Dark Corn Syrup
2   cups heavy cream, divided
1½ cups broken cookies (chocolate wafers
      or other crisp cookies)
1   cup coarsely chopped walnuts
      Chocolate, nuts and whipped cream
      (optional)

1. Line 12 (2½-inch) muffin pan cups with paper or foil liners.

2. In large heavy saucepan combine chocolate and corn syrup; stir over low heat just until chocolate melts. Remove from heat. Stir in ½ cup of the cream until blended.

3. Refrigerate 25 to 30 minutes or until cool. Stir in cookies and walnuts. In small bowl with mixer at medium speed, beat remaining 1½ cups cream until soft peaks form; gently fold into chocolate mixture just until combined. Spoon into prepared muffin pan cups.

4. Freeze 4 to 6 hours or until firm. Let stand at room temperature several minutes before serving. If desired, garnish with chocolate, nuts or whipped cream. Store covered in freezer for up to 1 month.

Makes 12 servings

Tortoni Squares: Spread mixture in 9-inch square pan. Freeze as above. Let stand; cut into 9 squares.

Classic Chocolate Pudding

    2 bars (1 ounce each) HERSHEY'S
       Unsweetened Baking Chocolate,
       broken into pieces
 2½ cups milk, divided
    1 cup sugar
  ¼ cup cornstarch
  ½ teaspoon salt
    3 egg yolks, slightly beaten
    1 tablespoon butter (do *not* use
       margarine)
    1 teaspoon vanilla extract
       Sweetened whipped cream (optional)
       Pecan halves (optional)

In medium saucepan, combine chocolate and 1½ cups
milk; cook over low heat, stirring constantly with
whisk, until chocolate is melted and mixture is
smooth. In medium bowl, stir together sugar,
cornstarch and salt; blend in remaining 1 cup milk and
egg yolks. Gradually stir into chocolate mixture. Cook
over medium heat, stirring constantly, until mixture
comes to a boil; boil 1 minute, stirring constantly.
Remove from heat; add butter and vanilla. Pour into
bowl; press plastic wrap directly onto surface.
Refrigerate 2 to 3 hours or until cold. Just before
serving, garnish with whipped cream and pecans, if
desired.   *Makes 4 to 6 servings*

Luscious Cold Chocolate Soufflés

1 envelope unflavored gelatin
¼ cup cold water
2 tablespoons reduced-calorie tub
   margarine
1½ cups cold skim milk, divided
½ cup sugar
⅓ cup HERSHEY₅S Cocoa or
   HERSHEY₅S European Style Cocoa
2½ teaspoons vanilla extract, divided
1 envelope (1.3 ounces) dry whipped
   topping mix

Measure lengths of foil to fit around 6 small soufflé
dishes (about 4 ounces each); fold in thirds lengthwise.
Tape securely to outside of dishes to form collar,
allowing collar to extend 1 inch above rims of dishes.
Lightly oil inside of foil.

In small microwave-safe bowl, sprinkle gelatin over
water; let stand 2 minutes to soften. Microwave at
HIGH (100%) 40 seconds; stir thoroughly. Stir in
margarine until melted; let stand 2 minutes or until
gelatin is completely dissolved. In small mixer bowl,
stir together 1 cup milk, sugar, cocoa and 2 teaspoons
vanilla. Beat on low speed of electric mixer while
gradually pouring in gelatin mixture. Beat until well
blended. Prepare topping mix as directed on package,
using remaining ½ cup milk and remaining ½ teaspoon
vanilla; carefully fold into chocolate mixture until well
blended.

Spoon into prepared soufflé dishes, filling ½-inch from top of collars. Cover; refrigerate until firm, about 3 hours. Carefully remove foil.   *Makes 6 servings*

Note: Six (6-ounce) custard cups may be used in place of soufflé dishes; omit foil collar.

Tiramisu

- 2 **packages (8 ounces each) cream cheese, softened**
- ⅔ **cup sugar**
- ¼ **cup Marsala wine**
- 2 **teaspoons vanilla extract**
- 2 **cups whipping cream, whipped**
- 1 **cup strong coffee or espresso, chilled**
- 2 **tablespoons almond liqueur** *or* **1 teaspoon almond extract**
- 2 **packages (3 ounces each) ladyfingers (24 ladyfingers)**
- 1 **cup HEATH® Bits**

In a mixing bowl, beat cream cheese and sugar until light. Blend in wine and vanilla. Fold in whipped cream. In a small bowl or measuring cup, combine coffee and liqueur. To assemble, split each ladyfinger in half horizontally and vertically. Place four pieces in each of eight footed dessert or wine glasses. Drizzle ladyfingers with the coffee mixture. Top with about ¼ cup cream mixture and several teaspoons HEATH® Bits. Repeat with two more layers ending with HEATH® Bits. Cover and refrigerate at least 2 hours before serving.   *Makes 8 servings*

Quick Chocolate Mousse

- 2 **cups heavy or whipping cream**
- 1 **envelope unflavored gelatin**
- ¼ **cup water**
- ⅓ **cup KARO® Light Corn Syrup**
- 1 **cup (6 ounces) semisweet chocolate chips**
- 1 **teaspoon vanilla**
- ¼ **teaspoon salt**

1. In large bowl with mixer at high speed, beat cream until soft peaks form.

2. In 1-quart saucepan sprinkle gelatin over water; let stand 1 minute. Add corn syrup. Stir over low heat until gelatin is completely dissolved, about 5 minutes. Remove from heat. Stir in chocolate chips, vanilla and salt until chocolate is melted.

3. Gently fold chocolate mixture into whipped cream. Spoon into individual serving dishes. Refrigerate.

Makes 8 servings

Fat-Free Cappuccino Flan

1   cup EGG BEATERS® Healthy Real Egg
      Product
½ cup sugar
1   tablespoon instant espresso or coffee
      powder
½ teaspoon vanilla extract
⅛ teaspoon ground cinnamon
2⅓ cups skim milk, scalded and cooled
      10 minutes
      Light nondairy whipped topping and
         cocoa powder or additional ground
         cinnamon, optional

In medium bowl, combine EGG BEATERS®, sugar,
espresso or coffee powder, vanilla and cinnamon.
Gradually stir in milk. Pour into 6 lightly greased
(6-ounce) custard cups or ramekins. Set cups in pan
filled with 1-inch depth hot water.

Bake at 350°F for 35 to 40 minutes or until knife
inserted in centers comes out clean. Remove cups from
pan; cool to room temperature. Chill until firm, about
2 hours. To serve, loosen edges with knife; invert onto
individual plates. Top with whipped topping and cocoa
or cinnamon if desired.   *Makes 6 servings*

Caramel Flan

1 cup sugar, divided
2 cups half-and-half
1 cup milk
1½ teaspoons vanilla extract
6 eggs
2 egg yolks
Hot water
Fresh whole and sliced strawberries
   (optional)

1. Preheat oven to 325°F. Heat 5½- to 6-cup ring mold in oven 10 minutes or until hot.

2. Heat ½ cup sugar in heavy, medium skillet over medium-high heat, stirring frequently, 5 to 8 minutes or until sugar is completely melted and deep amber in color. *Do not allow sugar to burn.*

3. Immediately pour caramelized sugar into ring mold. Holding mold with potholder, quickly rotate to coat bottom and sides evenly with sugar. Place mold on wire rack. (**Caution:** Caramelized sugar is very hot; do not touch it.)

4. Combine half-and-half and milk in heavy 2-quart saucepan. Heat over medium heat until almost simmering; remove from heat. Add remaining ½ cup sugar and vanilla, stirring until sugar is dissolved.

5. Lightly beat eggs and egg yolks in large bowl until blended but not foamy; gradually stir in milk mixture. Pour custard into ring mold. Place mold in large baking pan; pour ½ inch hot water into baking pan.

6. Bake 35 to 40 minutes until knife inserted into center of custard comes out clean. Remove mold from water bath; place on wire rack. Let stand 30 minutes. Cover and refrigerate 1½ to 2 hours until thoroughly chilled.

7. To serve, loosen inner and outer edges of flan with tip of small knife. Cover mold with rimmed serving plate; invert and lift off mold. Garnish with strawberries, if desired. Spoon some of the melted caramel over each serving.   *Makes 6 to 8 servings*

Caramel Sundaes

> 1   **cup 1% low-fat milk**
> 1   **tablespoon cornstarch**
> 1   **tablespoon margarine**
> ½   **cup firmly packed dark brown sugar**
> 1   **teaspoon vanilla extract**
> 1   **pint vanilla ice milk or nonfat frozen
>   yogurt, divided**

1. Combine milk and cornstarch in heavy saucepan. Stir until cornstarch is completely dissolved. Add margarine and brown sugar; cook over medium-low heat, stirring constantly with wire whisk. Bring to a boil. Boil 1 minute. Remove from heat; stir in vanilla. Cool to room temperature.

2. Place ½ cup ice milk in each of four sherbet glasses. Top each with ¼ cup caramel sauce.

Makes 4 servings

Chocolate Lovers'

DELIGHTS

Chocolate Truffle Mousse

1   cup whipping cream, divided
1   egg yolk
2   tablespoons corn syrup
2   tablespoons margarine or butter
4   squares (1 ounce each) semisweet
      chocolate, coarsely chopped
4   squares (1 ounce each) milk chocolate,
      coarsely chopped
5   teaspoons powdered sugar
½   teaspoon vanilla
     Sweetened whipped cream, fresh
        raspberries and mint leaves
        (optional)

1. Whisk ½ cup cream, egg yolk, corn syrup and
margarine in medium heavy saucepan over medium
heat until mixture simmers. Continue whisking while
mixture simmers 2 minutes. Remove from heat; add
chocolates, stirring until smooth. Cool to room
temperature.

2. Beat remaining ½ cup cream in medium bowl with
electric mixer at high speed until soft peaks form. Add
powdered sugar and vanilla; beat until stiff peaks form.

3. Stir whipped cream into chocolate mixture. Pour
into medium serving bowl. Chill 4 hours or overnight.
Garnish with sweetened whipped cream, fresh
strawberries and mint leaves, if desired.

Makes 6 servings

Decadent Chocolate Mousse

1¼ cups semisweet chocolate chips, divided
2 cups chilled whipping cream, divided
5 egg yolks
1 teaspoon vanilla extract
¼ cup sugar
1½ teaspoons butter or margarine

1. Heat 1 cup chocolate chips in medium saucepan over low heat until melted, stirring frequently. Remove from heat and stir in ¼ cup whipping cream.

2. Place egg yolks in medium bowl. Whisk about half of chocolate mixture into egg yolks; whisk egg yolk mixture back into chocolate mixture in saucepan. Cook over low heat 2 minutes, whisking constantly. Remove from heat; cool 3 to 5 minutes.

3. Beat remaining 1¾ cups whipping cream and vanilla to soft peaks in medium bowl. Gradually beat in sugar; continue beating until stiff peaks form. Stir about one-fourth of whipped cream into chocolate mixture; fold chocolate mixture into remaining whipped cream until completely combined.

4. Pour mousse into serving bowl or individual dessert dishes; cover and refrigerate 8 hours or until set. (Mousse may be refrigerated up to 2 days.)

5. Heat remaining ¼ cup chocolate chips in small saucepan over very low heat until melted; stir in butter until smooth. Spoon mixture into small resealable plastic food storage bag. Cut small corner off bottom of bag with scissors. Pipe designs on waxed paper-lined plate; refrigerate 15 minutes or until firm. (Designs may be refrigerated up to 3 days.)

6. To complete recipe, carefully peel waxed paper from chocolate designs; place on mousse before serving.

Makes 6 servings

Chocolate Lover's Mousse for Two

     2 tablespoons sugar
     ½ teaspoon unflavored gelatin
     ¼ cup milk
     ½ cup HERSHEY'S MINI CHIPS®
        Semi-Sweet Chocolate
     1 tablespoon orange-flavored liqueur, rum
        or 1 teaspoon vanilla extract
     ½ cup cold whipping cream
        Additional whipped cream (optional)

In small saucepan, stir together sugar and gelatin; stir in milk. Let stand 2 minutes to soften gelatin. Cook over medium heat, stirring constantly, until mixture begins to boil. Remove from heat. Immediately add small chocolate chips; stir until melted. Stir in liqueur; cool to room temperature. In small bowl on high speed of electric mixer, beat whipping cream until stiff. Gradually fold in chocolate mixture. Spoon into serving dishes. Refrigerate before serving. Garnish with additional whipped cream, if desired.

Makes 2 servings

Chocolate Mousse Torte

⅔ cup butter or margarine, softened
1 cup sugar
3 eggs
1½ teaspoons vanilla extract
2 cups all-purpose flour
⅔ cup HERSHEY₅S Cocoa or
   HERSHEY₅S European Style Cocoa
1½ teaspoons baking powder
½ teaspoon baking soda
1⅓ cups milk
Chocolate Mousse Filling
(recipe follows)

Heat oven to 350°F. Line 15½×10½×1-inch jelly-roll
pan with foil; grease and flour foil. In large bowl, beat
butter and sugar until creamy. Add eggs and vanilla;
beat well. Stir together flour, cocoa, baking powder and
baking soda; add to butter mixture alternately with
milk, beating well after each addition. Spread batter
into prepared pan. Bake 15 to 20 minutes or until
wooden pick inserted in center comes out clean. Cool
cake in pan 10 minutes. Invert onto wire rack; carefully
peel off foil. Cool completely. Prepare Chocolate
Mousse Filling. Trim cake edges; cut cake crosswise
into four equal pieces, each about 10×3½ inches. Place
one layer on serving plate; spread with about ½ cup
filling. Repeat with two more layers and filling; pipe or
spread remaining filling on fourth layer. Refrigerate
until ready to serve. Cover; refrigerate leftover cake.

Makes 10 to 12 servings

Chocolate Mousse Filling

1 teaspoon unflavored gelatin
1 tablespoon cold water
2 tablespoons boiling water
1 cup (½ pint) cold whipping cream
⅓ cup powdered sugar
3 tablespoons HERSHEY'S Cocoa or
    HERSHEY'S European Style Cocoa
1 teaspoon vanilla extract

In small cup, sprinkle gelatin over cold water; let stand 2 minutes to soften. Add boiling water; stir until gelatin is completely dissolved and mixture is clear. Cool 5 minutes. In large bowl on high speed of electric mixer, beat whipping cream, powdered sugar, cocoa and vanilla until thickened. Add gelatin mixture; beat until stiff. Use immediately.

Chocolate Dream Torte

1 package DUNCAN HINES® Moist Deluxe Dark Chocolate Fudge Cake Mix
1 package (6 ounces) semi-sweet chocolate chips, melted, for garnish
1 container (8 ounces) frozen whipped topping, thawed and divided
1 container (16 ounces) DUNCAN HINES® Creamy Homestyle Milk Chocolate Frosting
3 tablespoons finely chopped dry roasted pistachios

1. Preheat oven to 350°F. Grease and flour two 9-inch round cake pans.

2. Prepare, bake and cool cake following package directions for Basic Recipe.

3. For chocolate hearts garnish, spread melted chocolate to ⅛-inch thickness on waxed-paper-lined baking sheet. Cut shapes with heart cookie cutter when chocolate begins to set. Refrigerate until firm. Push out heart shapes. Set aside.

4. To assemble, split each cake layer in half horizontally. Place one split cake layer on serving plate. Spread one-third whipped topping on top. Repeat with remaining layers and whipped topping, leaving top plain. Frost sides and top with Milk Chocolate frosting. Sprinkle pistachios on top. Position chocolate hearts by pushing points down into cake. Refrigerate until ready to serve.   *Makes 12 servings*

Double Chocolate Delight

3 tablespoons butter or margarine,
  melted
2 tablespoons sugar
1 cup graham cracker crumbs
½ cup milk
1 HERSHEY'S Milk Chocolate Bar
  (7 ounces), broken into pieces
½ cup HERSHEY'S MINI CHIPS® Semi-
  Sweet Chocolate
1 cup (½ pint) cold whipping cream
  Sweetened whipped cream
  Sliced sweetened strawberries

In small bowl, stir together butter and sugar. Add
graham cracker crumbs; mix well. Press mixture firmly
onto bottom of 8-inch square pan. Refrigerate 1 to
2 hours or until firm. Meanwhile, in small saucepan,
heat milk just until it begins to boil; remove from heat.
Immediately add chocolate bar pieces and small
chocolate chips; stir until chocolate melts and mixture
is smooth. Pour into medium bowl; cool to room
temperature. In small bowl on high speed of electric
mixer, beat whipping cream until stiff; fold gently into
chocolate mixture. Pour onto prepared crust; freeze
several hours or until firm. Cut into squares. Just
before serving, garnish with sweetened whipped cream
and strawberries.   *Makes 6 to 8 servings*

KAHLÚA® Chocolate Decadence

½ cup butter
8 ounces (8 squares) semisweet baking
    chocolate, divided
3 extra large eggs
¾ cup granulated sugar
1¼ cups finely ground walnuts or pecans
2 tablespoons all-purpose flour
5 tablespoons KAHLÚA® Liqueur, divided
1 teaspoon vanilla
    Sifted powdered sugar
    Raspberries for garnish

Preheat oven to 325°F. In small saucepan over medium
heat, melt butter and 6 ounces chocolate, stirring until
blended. Remove from heat; cool. In large bowl, beat
eggs and granulated sugar at high speed of electric
mixer about 3 minutes or until light and lemon
colored. Stir together walnuts and flour; gradually beat
into egg mixture.

Stir 3 tablespoons KAHLÚA® and vanilla into cooled
chocolate mixture; gradually beat into egg mixture
until well combined. Pour batter into 9-inch
springform pan. Bake 35 to 45 minutes or until top
is set. Cool cake in pan.

Remove side of pan; place cake on serving plate.
Sprinkle top with powdered sugar. Melt remaining
2 ounces chocolate. Stir together melted chocolate and
remaining 2 tablespoons KAHLÚA®; drizzle over cake.
Decorate with raspberries, if desired.

Makes one 9-inch cake

Chocolate Lover's Cheesecake

Graham Crust (recipe follows)
2 packages (8 ounces each) cream
   cheese, softened
¾ cup plus 2 tablespoons sugar, divided
½ cup HERSHEY'S Cocoa
2 teaspoons vanilla extract, divided
2 eggs
1 cup HERSHEY'S Semi-Sweet
   Chocolate Chips
1 container (8 ounces) dairy sour cream

Prepare Graham Crust. Heat oven to 375°F. In large
bowl, beat cream cheese, ¾ cup sugar, cocoa and
1 teaspoon vanilla until light and fluffy. Add eggs; beat
until well blended. Stir in chocolate chips. Pour into
prepared crust. Bake 20 minutes. Remove from oven;
cool 15 minutes. *Increase oven temperature to 425°F.*
In small bowl, stir together sour cream, remaining
2 tablespoons sugar and remaining 1 teaspoon vanilla;
stir until smooth. Spread over baked filling. Bake
10 minutes. Remove from oven to wire rack. With
knife, loosen cake from side of pan. Cool completely;
remove side of pan. Refrigerate several hours or until
cold. Cover; refrigerate leftover cheesecake.

Makes 10 to 12 servings

Graham Crust: In medium bowl, stir together 1½
cups graham cracker crumbs and ⅓ cup sugar. Add
⅓ cup melted butter or margarine; mix well. Press
mixture firmly onto bottom and halfway up side of
9-inch springform pan.

Chocolate Truffle Tart

CRUST
- ⅔ cup all-purpose flour
- ½ cup powdered sugar
- ½ cup ground walnuts
- 6 tablespoons (¾ stick) butter or margarine, softened
- ⅓ cup NESTLÉ® TOLL HOUSE® Baking Cocoa

FILLING
- 1¼ cups heavy whipping cream
- ¼ cup granulated sugar
- 2 cups (12-ounce package) NESTLÉ® TOLL HOUSE® Semi-Sweet Chocolate Morsels
- 2 tablespoons seedless raspberry jam
  Sweetened whipped cream (optional)
  Fresh raspberries (optional)

FOR CRUST:

BEAT flour, powdered sugar, nuts, butter and cocoa in large mixer bowl until soft dough forms. Press dough onto bottom and up side of ungreased 9- or 9½-inch fluted tart pan with removeable bottom.

BAKE in preheated 350°F oven for 12 to 14 minutes or until puffed. Cool completely in pan on wire rack.

FOR FILLING:
COMBINE cream and granulated sugar in medium saucepan. Bring just to a boil, stirring occasionally. Remove from heat. Stir in morsels and jam; let stand for 5 minutes. Whisk until smooth. Transfer to small mixer bowl. Cover; chill for 45 to 60 minutes or until mixture is cooled and slightly thickened.

BEAT for 20 to 30 seconds or just until color lightens slightly. Spoon into crust. Chill until firm. Remove rim of pan; garnish with whipped cream and raspberries.

Makes 8 servings

Chocolate Truffle Cake Supreme

1¼ cups (2½ sticks) butter (do *not* use margarine)
¾ cup HERSHEY'S Cocoa
1 cup plus 1 tablespoon sugar, divided
1 tablespoon all-purpose flour
2 teaspoons vanilla extract
4 eggs, separated
1 cup (½ pint) cold whipping cream

Heat oven to 425°F. Grease bottom of 8-inch springform pan. In medium saucepan over low heat, melt butter. Add cocoa and 1 cup sugar; stir until well blended. Remove from heat; cool slightly. Stir in flour and vanilla. Add egg yolks, one at a time, beating well after each addition. In medium bowl on high speed of electric mixer, beat egg whites with remaining 1 tablespoon sugar until soft peaks form; gradually fold into chocolate mixture. Spread batter into prepared pan. Bake 16 to 18 minutes or until edge is firm. (Center will be soft.) Cool completely in pan on wire rack. (Cake will sink slightly in center as it cools.) Remove side of pan. Refrigerate cake at least 6 hours. In small bowl on high speed, beat whipping cream until stiff; spread over top of cake. Cut cake while cold, but let stand at room temperature 10 to 15 minutes before serving.   *Makes 10 servings*

Chocolate Bavarian Pie

1   **envelope unflavored gelatin**
1¾ **cups milk, divided**
⅔   **cup sugar**
6   **tablespoons HERSHEY'S Cocoa**
1   **tablespoon light corn syrup**
2   **tablespoons butter (do *not* use
      margarine)**
¾   **teaspoon vanilla extract**
1   **cup (½ pint) cold whipping cream**
1   **baked 9-inch pie crust or crumb crust**

In medium saucepan, sprinkle gelatin over 1 cup milk;
let stand 2 minutes to soften. Stir together sugar and
cocoa. Add to mixture in saucepan. Add corn syrup.
Cook, stirring constantly, until mixture comes to a
boil. Remove from heat. Add butter; stir until melted.
Blend in ¾ cup milk and vanilla. Pour into large mixer
bowl. Cool; refrigerate until almost set. In small bowl
on high speed of electric mixer, beat whipping cream
until stiff. Beat chocolate mixture on medium speed of
electric mixer until smooth. On low speed, add half the
whipped cream to chocolate mixture, beating just until
blended. Pour into prepared crust. Refrigerate 3 hours
or until firm. Just before serving, garnish with
remaining whipped cream. Cover and refrigerate
leftover pie.   *Makes 6 to 8 servings*

Hot Fudge Sundae Cake

1   package DUNCAN HINES® Moist
     Deluxe Dark Chocolate Fudge
     Cake Mix
½   gallon brick vanilla ice cream

FUDGE SAUCE

1   can (12 ounces) evaporated milk
1¾ cups sugar
4   squares (1 ounce each) unsweetened
     chocolate
¼   cup butter or margarine
1½ teaspoons vanilla extract
¼   teaspoon salt
     Whipped cream, for garnish
     Maraschino cherries, for garnish

1. Preheat oven to 350°F. Grease and flour
13×9×2-inch pan. Prepare, bake and cool cake
following package directions.

2. Remove cake from pan. Split cake in half
horizontally. Place bottom layer back in pan. Cut ice
cream into even slices and place evenly over bottom
cake layer (use all the ice cream). Place remaining cake
layer over ice cream. Cover and freeze.

3. For sauce, combine evaporated milk and sugar in
medium saucepan. Stir constantly on medium heat
until mixture comes to a rolling boil. Boil and stir for
1 minute. Add unsweetened chocolate and stir until
melted. Beat over heat until smooth. Remove from
heat. Stir in butter, vanilla extract and salt.

4. Cut cake into serving squares. Spoon hot fudge sauce on top of each cake square. Garnish with whipped cream and a maraschino cherry.

Makes 12 to 16 servings

Tip: Fudge sauce may be prepared ahead and refrigerated in tightly sealed jar. Reheat before serving.

Chocolate Plunge

⅔ cup KARO® Light or Dark Corn Syrup
½ cup heavy cream
8 squares (1 ounce each) semisweet chocolate
   Assorted fresh fruit

1. In medium saucepan combine corn syrup and cream. Bring to boil over medium heat. Remove from heat.

2. Add chocolate; stir until completely melted.

3. Serve warm as a dip for fruit.   *Makes 1½ cups*

Note: Chocolate Plunge can be made a day ahead. Store covered in refrigerator. Reheat before serving.

Try some of these "dippers:" Candied pineapple, dried apricots, waffle squares, ladyfingers, macaroons, pretzels, croissants, mint cookies or peanut butter cookies.

Microwave Directions: In medium microwavable bowl combine corn syrup and cream. Microwave on HIGH (100%), 1½ minutes or until boiling. Add chocolate; stir until completely melted. Serve as directed.

Chocolate Bread Pudding

4 squares (1 ounce each) semisweet
  chocolate
½ cup KARO® Light or Dark Corn Syrup
¼ cup sugar
¼ teaspoon cinnamon
¼ teaspoon salt
1 cup milk
2 eggs, lightly beaten
3 cups fresh white bread cubes (about
  7 slices)
¼ cup chopped walnuts (optional)
  Vanilla Custard Sauce (recipe follows)

1. Preheat oven to 375°F. Grease 1½-quart casserole
dish.

2. In large saucepan combine chocolate, corn syrup,
sugar, cinnamon and salt; stir over low heat just until
chocolate melts. Remove from heat; stir in milk until
blended. Stir in eggs and bread cubes; let stand
5 minutes. Pour into prepared dish. If desired, sprinkle
with walnuts.

3. Bake 30 to 35 minutes or until knife inserted in
center comes out clean. Serve warm with Vanilla
Custard Sauce.   *Makes 6 to 8 servings*

Vanilla Custard Sauce

  2   tablespoons sugar
  1   tablespoon ARGO® or KINGSFORD'S®
     Corn Starch
1½ cups milk
  ¼ cup KARO® Light Corn Syrup
  1   egg yolk, slightly beaten
  ½ teaspoon vanilla

1. In 2-quart saucepan combine sugar and corn starch. Gradually stir in milk until smooth. Stir in corn syrup and egg yolk.

2. Stirring constantly, bring to boil over medium-low heat and boil 1 minute. Remove from heat. Stir in vanilla.   *Makes about 1½ cups*

Hot Chocolate Soufflé

¾ cup HERSHEY®S Cocoa
1 cup sugar, divided
½ cup all-purpose flour
¼ teaspoon salt
2 cups milk
6 egg yolks, well beaten
2 tablespoons butter or margarine
1 teaspoon vanilla extract
8 egg whites
¼ teaspoon cream of tartar
   Sweetened whipped cream

Adjust oven rack to lowest position. Heat oven to 350°F. Lightly butter 2½-quart soufflé dish; sprinkle with sugar. For collar, cut a length of heavy-duty foil to fit around soufflé dish; fold in thirds lengthwise. Lightly butter one side of foil. Attach foil, buttered side in, around outside of dish allowing foil to extend at least 2 inches above dish. Secure foil with tape or string.

In large saucepan, stir together cocoa, ¾ cup sugar, flour and salt; gradually stir in milk. Cook over medium heat, stirring constantly with wire whisk, until mixture boils; remove from heat. Gradually stir small amount of chocolate mixture into beaten egg yolks; blend well. Add egg mixture to chocolate mixture in pan, blending well. Cook and stir 1 minute. Add butter and vanilla, stirring until blended. Set aside; cool 20 minutes. In large bowl, beat egg whites with cream of tartar until soft peaks form; gradually add remaining ¼ cup sugar, beating until stiff peaks form. Gently fold about one third of beaten egg white mixture into chocolate mixture. Lightly fold chocolate mixture, half at a time, into remaining beaten egg white mixture just until blended; do not overfold.

Gently pour mixture into prepared dish; smooth top with spatula. Gently place dish in larger baking pan; pour hot water into larger pan to depth of 1 inch.

Bake 65 to 70 minutes or until puffed and set. Remove soufflé dish from water. Carefully remove foil. Serve immediately with sweetened whipped cream.

Makes 8 to 10 servings

Hot Chocolate Fudge Sauce

¾ **cup sugar**
¾ **cup heavy or whipping cream**
½ **cup KARO® Light Corn Syrup**
2 **tablespoons MAZOLA® Margarine or butter**
1 **package (8 ounces) semisweet chocolate**
1 **teaspoon vanilla**

1. In large saucepan combine sugar, cream, corn syrup and margarine. Stirring constantly, bring to full boil over medium heat. Remove from heat. Stir in chocolate until melted. Stir in vanilla.

2. Serve warm over ice cream. Store in refrigerator.

Makes about 2¼ cups

Chocolate Coconut Balls

3 bars (1 ounce each) HERSHEY¿S
   Unsweetened Baking Chocolate,
   broken into pieces
¼ cup (½ stick) butter (do *not* use
   margarine)
½ cup sweetened condensed milk (*not*
   evaporated milk)
¾ cup granulated sugar
¼ cup water
1 tablespoon light corn syrup
1 teaspoon vanilla extract
2 cups MOUNDS® Sweetened Coconut
   Flakes
1 cup chopped nuts
   Powdered sugar

In large heavy saucepan over low heat, melt chocolate
and butter. Add sweetened condensed milk; stir to
blend. Remove from heat. In small heavy saucepan, stir
together granulated sugar, water and corn syrup. Cook
over medium heat, stirring constantly, until sugar is
dissolved. Cook, without stirring, until mixture
reaches 250°F on candy thermometer or until syrup,
when dropped into very cold water, forms a firm ball
that does not flatten when removed from water. (Bulb
of thermometer should not rest on bottom of
saucepan.) Remove from heat; stir into chocolate
mixture. Add vanilla, coconut and nuts; stir until well
blended. Refrigerate about 30 minutes or until firm

enough to handle. Shape into 1-inch balls; roll in
powdered sugar. Store in tightly covered container in
cool, dry place.   *Makes about 5 dozen candies*

Note: For best results, do *not* double this recipe.

Fudgy Banana Rocky Road Clusters

    1 **package (12 ounces) semisweet
          chocolate chips**
    ⅓ **cup crunchy or creamy peanut butter**
    3 **cups miniature marshmallows**
    1 **cup dried banana chips**
    1 **cup unsalted peanuts**

1. Place chocolate chips and peanut butter in large
microwavable bowl. Microwave at HIGH 2 minutes or
until chips are melted and mixture is smooth, stirring
twice.

2. Fold in marshmallows, banana chips and peanuts.

3. Line baking sheets with waxed paper. Grease waxed
paper.

4. Drop rounded tablespoonfuls chocolate mixture
onto prepared baking sheets; refrigerate until firm.

5. Store in airtight container in refrigerator.
                    Makes 2½ to 3 dozen clusters

Variations: Assorted dried fruits can be substituted for
the banana chips in this recipe. Try dried apricots or
cherries for a unique taste sensation.

Double Chocolate Truffles

½ cup whipping cream
1 tablespoon butter or margarine
4 bars (1 ounce each) HERSHEY®S
     Semi-Sweet Baking Chocolate,
     broken into pieces
1 HERSHEY®S Milk Chocolate Bar
     (7 ounces), broken into pieces
1 tablespoon amaretto (almond-flavored
     liqueur) *or* ¼ to ½ teaspoon almond
     extract
   Ground almonds

In small saucepan, combine whipping cream and butter. Cook over medium heat, stirring constantly, just until mixture is very hot. *Do not boil.* Remove from heat; add chocolate, chocolate bar pieces and liqueur. Stir with whisk until smooth. Press plastic wrap directly onto surface; cool several hours or until mixture is firm enough to handle. Shape into 1-inch balls; roll in almonds to coat. Refrigerate until firm, about 2 hours. Store in tightly covered container in refrigerator.　　　　*Makes about 2 dozen candies*

Easy Luscious Fudge

- 2 cups (12 ounces) semisweet chocolate chips
- ¾ cup milk chocolate chips
- 2 squares (1 ounce each) unsweetened chocolate, coarsely chopped
- 1 can (14 ounces) sweetened condensed milk
- 1 cup mini marshmallows
- ½ cup chopped walnuts (optional)

1. Line 8-inch square pan with foil, extending 1-inch over ends of pan. Lightly grease foil.

2. Melt chocolates in medium saucepan over low heat, stirring constantly. Remove from heat. Stir in condensed milk; add marshmallows and walnuts, if desired, stirring until combined.

3. Spread chocolate mixture evenly in prepared pan. Score into 2-inch triangles by cutting halfway through fudge with sharp knife while fudge is still warm.

4. Refrigerate until firm. Remove from pan by lifting fudge and foil. Place on cutting board; cut along score lines into triangles. Remove foil. Store in airtight container in refrigerator.

Makes about 3 dozen pieces fudge

Mint Fudge: Substitute 1⅔ cups (10 ounces) mint chocolate chips for semisweet chips and ½ cup chopped party mints for walnuts.

Fast 'n' Fabulous Dark Chocolate Fudge

½ cup KARO® Light or Dark Corn Syrup
⅓ cup evaporated milk
3 cups (18 ounces) semisweet chocolate chips
¾ cup confectioners sugar, sifted
2 teaspoons vanilla
1 cup coarsely chopped nuts (optional)

1. Grease 8- or 9-inch square baking pan.

2. In 2-quart saucepan combine corn syrup and evaporated milk. Add chocolate. Stirring constantly, cook over medium-low heat until chocolate melts. Remove from heat.

3. Add confectioners sugar, vanilla and nuts. With wooden spoon beat until thick and glossy.

4. Spread in prepared pan. Refrigerate 2 hours or until firm. Cut into squares.   *Makes 25 squares*

Microwave Directions: Line 8- or 9-inch square pan with plastic wrap. In 3-quart microwavable bowl stir corn syrup and milk until smooth. Microwave on High (100%) 3 minutes. Stir in chocolate until melted. Complete as above.

Marvelous Marble Fudge: Omit nuts. Prepare as directed above; spread in prepared pan. Drop ⅓ cup SKIPPY® Creamy Peanut Butter over fudge in small dollops. With small spatula, swirl fudge to marbleize. Chill and cut as above.

Double Peanut Butter Chocolate Fudge: Prepare as directed. Stir in ⅓ cup SKIPPY® SUPER CHUNK® Peanut Butter. Spread in prepared pan. Drop additional ⅓ cup peanut butter over fudge in small dollops. With small spatula, swirl fudge to marbleize. Chill and cut as directed.

Peanut Butter Cups

- 20 large marshmallows
- ½ cup crunchy peanut butter
- 2 tablespoons margarine or butter
- 2 tablespoons milk
- 2 cups powdered sugar
- ⅔ cup chocolate corn puff cereal
- ¾ cup semisweet or milk chocolate chips, melted

1. Line 30 mini-muffin pan cups with mini-paper cups or lightly grease mini-muffin pan cups.

2. Place marshmallows, peanut butter, margarine and milk in medium microwavable bowl. Microwave at HIGH 1½ minutes; stir until smooth.

3. Stir in powdered sugar until blended. Add cereal; stir. Press tablespoonful of marshmallow mixture into each cup.

4. Spoon 1 teaspoonful of melted chocolate over top of each peanut butter cup. Refrigerate until firm. Store in airtight container in refrigerator.   *Makes 30 cups*

Chocolate Chip Cookie Dough Fudge

⅓ cup butter, melted

⅓ cup packed brown sugar

¾ cup all-purpose flour

½ teaspoon salt, divided

1⅓ cups mini semisweet chocolate chips, divided

1 package (1 pound) powdered sugar (about 4 cups)

1 package (8 ounces) cream cheese, softened

1 teaspoon vanilla extract

1. Line 8- or 9-inch square pan with foil, leaving 1-inch overhang on sides. Lightly butter foil.

2. Combine butter and brown sugar in small bowl. Stir in flour and ¼ teaspoon salt. Stir in ⅓ cup chips.

3. Form dough into a ball. Place on plastic wrap; flatten into a disc. Wrap disc in plastic wrap; freeze 10 minutes or until firm.

4. Unwrap dough; cut into ½-inch pieces with utility knife. Store in airtight container in refrigerator.

5. Place powdered sugar, cream cheese, vanilla and remaining ¼ teaspoon salt in large bowl. Beat with electric mixer at low speed until combined. Scrape down side of bowl; beat at medium speed until smooth.

6. Melt remaining 1 cup chips in heavy small saucepan over very low heat, stirring *constantly* to prevent scorching. Remove from heat as soon as chocolate is melted.

7. Add melted chocolate to cream cheese mixture; beat just until blended. Stir in chilled cookie dough pieces.

8. Spread evenly in prepared pan. Score into squares, about 1¼×1¼ inches, by cutting halfway through fudge with sharp knife.

9. Refrigerate until firm. Remove from pan by lifting fudge and foil using foil handles. Place on cutting board; cut along score lines into squares. Remove foil. Store in airtight container in refrigerator.

Makes about 3 to 4 dozen candies

Foolproof Dark Chocolate Fudge

3 cups (1½ packages, 12 ounces each) HERSHEY₀S Semi-Sweet Chocolate Chips
1 can (14 ounces) sweetened condensed milk (*not* evaporated milk)
Dash salt
1 cup chopped walnuts
1½ teaspoons vanilla extract

Line 8- or 9-inch square pan with foil, extending foil over edges of pan. In medium, heavy saucepan over low heat, melt chocolate chips with sweetened condensed milk and salt. Remove from heat; stir in walnuts and vanilla. Spread into prepared pan. Refrigerate 2 hours or until firm. Use foil to lift fudge from pan; peel off foil. Cut into squares. Store loosely covered at room temperature.

Makes about 5 dozen pieces or 2 pounds fudge

Just for the HOLIDAYS

Peppermint Fudge Pie

1 package (6 ounces) semisweet
    chocolate chips
2 cups miniature marshmallows
¼ cup milk or cream
2 tablespoons chocolate-mint liqueur
3 cups whipped cream, divided
1 (6-ounce) KEEBLER® READY-CRUST®
    Chocolate Flavored Pie Crust
2 tablespoons crushed peppermint
    candies or candy canes

In microwave-safe bowl, combine chocolate chips,
marshmallows and milk. Cook at MEDIUM (50%
power) 2 to 3 minutes, stirring twice, until smooth.
Stir in liqueur. Cool at room temperature. Fold in 1½
cups whipped cream. Spoon into pie shell. Fold
crushed candies into remaining 1½ cups whipped
cream. Spread over chocolate layer. Cover and freeze
until firm, about 3 hours. Pie may be made up to
several weeks ahead. Remove pie from freezer and
slice. Let stand 3 to 5 minutes before serving. Store
leftovers in freezer.   *Makes 8 servings*

Chocolate Mint Mousse Pie

1   teaspoon unflavored gelatin
1   tablespoon cold water
2   tablespoons boiling water
½   cup sugar
⅓   cup HERSHEY'S Cocoa or
     HERSHEY'S European Style Cocoa
1   cup (½ pint) cold whipping cream
1   teaspoon vanilla extract
1   baked 8- or 9-inch pie crust, cooled
     Mint Cream Topping (recipe follows)

In small cup, sprinkle gelatin over cold water; let stand
2 minutes to soften. Add boiling water; stir until
gelatin is completely dissolved and mixture is clear.
Cool slightly, about 5 minutes. Meanwhile, in medium
bowl, stir together sugar and cocoa; add whipping
cream and vanilla. Beat on medium speed of electric
mixer until stiff, scraping bottom of bowl occasionally.
Add gelatin mixture; beat just until blended. Pour into
prepared crust. Prepare Mint Cream Topping; spread
over filling. Refrigerate about 2 hours. Garnish as
desired. Cover; refrigerate leftover pie.

Makes 6 to 8 servings

Mint Cream Topping

1   cup (½ pint) cold whipping cream
2   tablespoons powdered sugar
¼   to ½ teaspoon peppermint extract
     Green food color

In medium bowl on medium speed of electric mixer, beat whipping cream, powdered sugar, peppermint extract and several drops green food color until stiff.

Apple Cranberry Pie

1   package (8 ounces) PHILADELPHIA
    BRAND® Cream Cheese, softened
½   cup firmly packed brown sugar, divided
1   egg
1   unbaked pastry shell (9 inch)
2   cups sliced peeled apples
½   cup halved cranberries
1   teaspoon ground cinnamon, divided
⅓   cup flour
⅓   cup old-fashioned or quick-cooking
    oats, uncooked
¼   cup (½ stick) butter or margarine
¼   cup chopped nuts

MIX cream cheese and ¼ cup of the sugar with electric mixer on medium speed until well blended. Blend in egg. Pour into pastry shell.

TOSS apples, cranberries and ½ teaspoon of the cinnamon. Spoon over cream cheese mixture.

MIX flour, oats, remaining ¼ cup sugar and ½ teaspoon cinnamon; cut in butter until mixture resembles coarse crumbs. Stir in nuts. Spoon over fruit mixture.

BAKE at 375°F for 40 to 45 minutes or until lightly browned. Cool slightly before serving.

Makes 8 to 10 servings

Linzer Torte

½ cup toasted whole almonds
1½ cups all-purpose flour
1 teaspoon ground cinnamon
¼ teaspoon salt
¾ cup granulated sugar
½ cup butter or margarine
½ teaspoon grated lemon peel
1 egg
¾ cup raspberry or apricot jam
Powdered sugar

1. Place almonds in food processor; process until almonds are ground, but not pasty. Measure enough to make ½ cup ground almonds.

2. Preheat oven to 375°F. Combine flour, almonds, cinnamon and salt in medium bowl; set aside.

3. Beat granulated sugar, butter and lemon peel in large bowl using electric mixer at medium speed about 5 minutes or until light and fluffy, scraping down side of bowl once. Beat in egg until well blended. Beat in flour mixture at low speed until well blended. Spoon ⅔ of dough onto bottom of 10-inch tart pan with removable bottom. Pat dough evenly over bottom and up side of pan. Spread jam over bottom of dough.

4. Roll remaining ⅓ of dough on lightly floured surface with lightly floured rolling pin into 10×6-inch rectangle. Cut dough into 10×½-inch strips. Arrange 4 to 5 strips of dough lengthwise across jam. Arrange another 4 to 5 strips of dough crosswise across top. Press ends of dough strips into edge of crust.

5. Bake 25 to 35 minutes until crust is golden brown. Cool completely in pan on wire rack. Remove from pan. Cut into wedges. Sprinkle with powdered sugar.

Makes 12 servings

Orange Pumpkin Tart

1½   cups all-purpose flour
1   cup QUAKER® Oats (quick or old fashioned, uncooked), divided
1   cup plus 2 tablespoons sugar, divided
¾   cup (1½ sticks) margarine
2   tablespoons water
1   can (16 ounces) pumpkin (1¾ cups)
1   egg white
1   teaspoon pumpkin pie spice
½   cup powdered sugar
2   teaspoons orange juice
½   teaspoon grated orange peel

Preheat oven to 400°F. Combine flour, ¾ cup oats and ½ cup sugar; cut in margarine until crumbly. Reserve ¾ cup oat mixture. Mix remaining oat mixture with water until dough is moistened. Divide into 2 parts; press each onto cookie sheet to form a 12×5-inch tart. Combine pumpkin, egg white, ½ cup sugar and pumpkin pie spice. Spread over tarts. Top with combined remaining ¼ cup oats, remaining 2 tablespoons sugar and reserved oat mixture. Bake 25 minutes or until golden. Cool. Drizzle with combined remaining ingredients. Refrigerate leftovers.

Makes 12 servings

Pumpkin Apple Tart

CRUST

- 1 cup plain dry bread crumbs
- 1 cup crunchy nut-like cereal nuggets
- ½ cup sugar
- ½ teaspoon ground cinnamon
- ½ teaspoon ground nutmeg
- ¼ cup MOTT'S® Natural Apple Sauce
- 2 tablespoons margarine, melted
- 1 egg white

FILLING

- 12 ounces evaporated skim milk
- 1½ cups solid-pack pumpkin
- ⅔ cup sugar
- ½ cup MOTT'S® Chunky Apple Sauce
- ⅓ cup GRANDMA'S® Molasses
- 2 egg whites
- 1 whole egg
- ½ teaspoon ground ginger
- ½ teaspoon ground cinnamon
- ½ teaspoon ground nutmeg
  Frozen light nondairy whipped topping, thawed (optional)

1. Preheat oven to 375°F. Spray 9- or 10-inch springform pan with nonstick cooking spray.

2. To prepare Crust, in medium bowl, combine bread crumbs, cereal, ½ cup sugar, ½ teaspoon cinnamon and ½ teaspoon nutmeg.

3. Add ¼ cup apple sauce, margarine and egg white; mix until moistened. Press onto bottom of prepared pan.

4. Bake 8 minutes.

5. To prepare Filling, place evaporated milk in small saucepan. Cook over medium heat until milk almost boils, stirring occasionally.

6. In large bowl, combine evaporated milk, pumpkin, ⅔ cup sugar, ½ cup apple sauce, molasses, 2 egg whites, whole egg, ginger, ½ teaspoon cinnamon and ½ teaspoon nutmeg. Pour into baked crust.

7. *Increase oven temperature to 400°F.* Bake 35 to 40 minutes or until center is set.

8. Cool 20 minutes on wire rack. Remove sides of pan. Spoon or pipe whipped topping onto tart, if desired. Cut into 12 slices. Refrigerate leftovers.

Makes 12 servings

Pumpkin Cheese-Swirled Pie

1 **package (3 ounces) cream cheese, softened**
½ **cup KARO® Light Corn Syrup, divided**
½ **teaspoon vanilla**
1 **cup canned solid pack pumpkin**
2 **eggs**
½ **cup evaporated milk**
¼ **cup sugar**
2 **teaspoons pumpkin pie spice**
¼ **teaspoon salt**
**Easy-As-Pie Crust (page 268) *or*
1 (9-inch) frozen deep-dish pie crust***

1. Preheat oven to 325°F.

2. In small bowl with mixer at medium speed, beat cream cheese until light and fluffy. Gradually beat in ¼ cup corn syrup and vanilla until smooth; set aside.

3. In medium bowl combine pumpkin, eggs, evaporated milk, remaining ¼ cup corn syrup, sugar, pumpkin pie spice and salt. Beat until smooth. Pour into pie crust.

4. Drop tablespoonfuls of cream cheese mixture onto pumpkin filling. With knife or small spatula, swirl mixture to give marbled effect.

5. Bake 50 to 60 minutes or until knife inserted halfway between edge and center comes out clean. Cool completely on wire rack. *Makes 8 servings*

*To use prepared frozen pie crust, do not thaw. Preheat oven and a cookie sheet. Pour filling into frozen crust. Bake on cookie sheet.

Low-Fat Pumpkin Cheesecake

⅓ cup graham cracker crumbs
1 can (16 ounces) solid pack pumpkin
2 cups low-fat ricotta cheese
1 cup sugar
3 tablespoons all-purpose flour
1 tablespoon nonfat dry milk powder
1 tablespoon ground cinnamon
1 teaspoon ground allspice
1 egg white
¾ cup canned evaporated skimmed milk
1 tablespoon vegetable oil
1 tablespoon vanilla extract

1. Preheat oven to 400°F. Spray 9-inch springform pan with nonstick cooking spray. Add graham cracker crumbs; shake to coat pan evenly. Set aside.

2. Combine pumpkin and ricotta cheese in food processor or blender; process until smooth. Add sugar, flour, milk powder, cinnamon, allspice, egg white, evaporated skimmed milk, oil and vanilla; process until smooth.

3. Pour mixture into prepared pan. Bake 15 minutes. *Reduce oven temperature to 275°F;* bake 1 hour and 15 minutes. Turn off oven; leave cheesecake in oven with door closed 1 hour. Remove from oven; cool completely on wire rack. Remove springform pan side. Cover cheesecake with plastic wrap; refrigerate at least 4 hours or up to 2 days. Garnish with fresh fruit, if desired. *Makes 16 servings*

PHILLY 3-STEP™ Double Layer Pumpkin Cheesecake

2 packages (8 ounces each)
PHILADELPHIA BRAND® Cream
Cheese, softened
½ cup sugar
½ teaspoon vanilla
2 eggs
½ cup canned pumpkin
½ teaspoon ground cinnamon
Dash *each* ground cloves and nutmeg
1 ready to use graham cracker pie crust
(6 ounces *or* 9 inch)

1. MIX cream cheese, sugar and vanilla with electric mixer on medium speed until well blended. Add eggs; mix until blended. In separate bowl, mix pumpkin and spices. Stir 1 cup of the cream cheese batter into pumpkin mixture.

2. POUR remaining cream cheese batter into crust. Top with pumpkin batter.

3. BAKE at 350°F for 40 minutes or until center is almost set. Cool. Refrigerate 3 hours or overnight. Garnish, if desired.   *Makes 8 servings*

Pumpkin Dessert Squares

3 cups gingersnap cookie crumbs
⅓ cup reduced-fat tablespread, melted
3 packages (8 ounces each)
   PHILADELPHIA BRAND® FREE®
   Fat Free Cream Cheese, softened
1½ cups sugar, divided
3 eggs, divided
1 teaspoon vanilla
1 can (16 ounces) pumpkin
1½ teaspoons pumpkin pie spice
1 can (12 ounces) evaporated skim milk

MIX crumbs and tablespread. Press into 13×9-inch baking pan.

BEAT cream cheese with electric mixer on medium speed until smooth. Add ¾ cup of the sugar, 2 of the eggs and vanilla, mixing until blended. Pour over crust.

BEAT remaining 1 egg in separate bowl. Stir in pumpkin, remaining ¾ cup sugar and pumpkin pie spice. Gradually stir in milk. Pour over cream cheese layer.

BAKE at 375°F for 1 hour or until set. Cool. Refrigerate until ready to serve. Garnish with COOL WHIP® LITE® Whipped Topping and additional cookie crumbs, if desired.   *Makes 20 servings*

Peppermint Cheesecake

CRUST
- 1¼ cups vanilla wafer crumbs
- 3 tablespoons melted margarine

FILLING
- 4 cups (30 ounces) SARGENTO® Light Ricotta Cheese
- ½ cup sugar
- ½ cup half-and-half
- ¼ cup all-purpose flour
- 1 teaspoon vanilla
- ¼ teaspoon salt
- 3 eggs
- 16 peppermint candies (½ cup crushed pieces)
  Fresh mint leaves (optional)

Lightly grease sides of 8- or 9-inch springform pan. Combine crumbs and margarine; mix well. Press evenly over bottom of pan. Refrigerate while preparing filling.

Combine ricotta cheese, sugar, half-and-half, flour, vanilla and salt in large bowl; beat with electric mixer until smooth. Add eggs, 1 at a time; beat until smooth. Place candies in heavy plastic bag. Crush with meat mallet or hammer. Reserve ¼ cup larger pieces for garnish; stir remaining crushed candies into batter. Pour batter over crust.

Bake at 350°F 1 hour or until center is just set. Turn off oven; cool in oven with door propped open 30 minutes. Remove to wire cooling rack; loosen cake from rim of pan with metal spatula. Cool completely; refrigerate at least 4 hours. Immediately before serving, garnish cake around top edge with reserved crushed candies and mint leaves, if desired.

Makes 8 servings

Cherry Cheesecake Squares

    2 cups graham cracker crumbs
    1 cup sugar, divided
    ¼ cup (½ stick) butter or margarine,
         melted
    3 packages (8 ounces each)
         PHILADELPHIA BRAND® Cream
         Cheese, softened
    1 teaspoon vanilla
    2 eggs
    1 can (20 ounces) cherry pie filling

MIX crumbs, ¼ cup of the sugar and butter. Press into 13×9-inch baking pan. Bake at 325°F for 10 minutes.

MIX cream cheese, remaining ¾ cup sugar and vanilla with electric mixer on medium speed until well blended. Add eggs; mix just until blended. Pour over crust.

BAKE at 325°F for 35 minutes or until center is almost set. Cool. Refrigerate 3 hours or overnight. Top with pie filling. Cut into squares. Garnish, if desired.

Makes 18 servings

PHILLY 3-STEP™ Caramel Apple Cheesecake

- 2 (8-ounce) packages PHILADELPHIA BRAND® Cream Cheese, softened
- ½ cup sugar
- ½ teaspoon vanilla
- 2 eggs
- ⅓ cup frozen apple juice concentrate, thawed
- 1 ready to use graham cracker pie crust (6 ounces *or* 9 inch)
- ¼ cup caramel ice cream topping
- ¼ cup chopped peanuts

1. MIX cream cheese, sugar and vanilla at medium speed with electric mixer until well blended. Add eggs; mix until blended. Blend in juice concentrate.

2. POUR into crust.

3. BAKE at 350°F, 40 minutes or until center is almost set. Cool. Refrigerate 3 hours or overnight. Drizzle with topping and sprinkle with peanuts before serving. Garnish with apple slices. *Makes 8 servings*

PHILLY 3-STEP™ Crème de Menthe Cheesecake

- 2 (8-ounce) packages PHILADELPHIA BRAND® Cream Cheese, softened
- ½ cup sugar
- ½ teaspoon vanilla
- 2 eggs
- 4 teaspoons green crème de menthe
- 1 ready to use chocolate flavored pie crust (6 ounces *or* 9 inch)

1. MIX cream cheese, sugar and vanilla at medium speed with electric mixer until well blended. Add eggs; mix until blended. Blend in crème de menthe.

2. POUR into crust.

3. BAKE at 350°F, 40 minutes or until center is almost set. Cool. Refrigerate 3 hours or overnight. Garnish with chocolate leaves and twigs.

Makes 8 servings

Mint Bon Bon Cheesecake: Substitute ¼ teaspoon peppermint extract and a few drops green food coloring for crème de menthe. Stir ½ cup mini semi-sweet chocolate chips into batter. Sprinkle with additional ¼ cup chips before baking.

Merri-Mint Truffles

1 package (10 ounces) mint chocolate
   chips
⅓ cup whipping cream
¼ cup butter or margarine
1 container (3½ ounces) chocolate
   sprinkles

1. Melt chocolate chips with cream and butter in heavy medium saucepan over low heat, stirring occasionally. Pour into pie pan. Refrigerate about 2 hours or until mixture is fudgy, but soft.

2. Shape about 1 tablespoonful of mixture into 1¼-inch ball. Repeat with remaining mixture. Roll balls in your palms to form uniform round shapes; place on waxed paper.

3. Place sprinkles in shallow bowl. Roll balls in sprinkles; place in petit four or candy cases. (If coating mixture won't stick because truffle has set, roll between your palms until outside is soft.) Store in airtight container up to 3 days in refrigerator or several weeks in freezer.   *Makes about 24 truffles*

Jolly Bourbon Balls

1 package (12 ounces) vanilla wafers,
   finely crushed (3 cups)
1 cup finely chopped nuts
1 cup powdered sugar, divided
1 cup (6 ounces) semisweet chocolate
   chips
½ cup light corn syrup
⅓ cup bourbon or rum

1. Combine crushed wafers, nuts and ½ cup powdered sugar in large bowl; set aside.

2. Melt chocolate with corn syrup in top of double boiler over simmering (not boiling) water. Stir in bourbon until smooth. Pour chocolate mixture over crumb mixture; stir to combine thoroughly. Shape scant 1 tablespoonful of mixture into 1-inch ball. Repeat with remaining mixture. Roll balls in your palms to form uniform round shapes; place on waxed paper.

3. Place remaining ½ cup powdered sugar in shallow bowl. Roll balls in powdered sugar; place in petit four or candy cases. Store in airtight containers at least 3 days before serving for flavors to mellow. (May be stored up to 2 weeks.)   *Makes about 48 candies*

Black Walnut Fudge

4 cups sugar
½ cup margarine
1 can (12 ounces) evaporated milk
3 tablespoons light corn syrup
1 pound vanilla milk chips*
1 jar (13 ounces) marshmallow creme
1 cup chopped black walnuts
1 tablespoon vanilla extract

*Do not use compound chocolate or confectioner's coating.

1. Line 13×9-inch pan with foil, leaving 1-inch overhang on sides. Lightly butter foil.

2. Combine sugar, margarine, evaporated milk and corn syrup in large saucepan; stir well. Bring to a boil over medium heat, stirring until sugar dissolves. Stop stirring.

3. Attach candy thermometer to side of pan, making sure bulb is completely submerged in sugar mixture but not touching bottom of pan.

4. Continue heating, without stirring, until mixture reaches soft-ball stage (234°F) on candy thermometer.

5. Remove from heat and add vanilla milk chips. Stir with wooden spoon until melted. Add marshmallow creme, walnuts and vanilla, beating well after each addition.

6. Pour into prepared pan. Score into squares by cutting halfway through fudge with sharp knife while fudge is still warm.

7. Remove from pan by lifting fudge and foil using foil handles. Place on cutting board. Cool completely. Cut along score lines into squares. Remove foil. Store in airtight container in refrigerator.

Makes about 3 pounds

Eggnog Gift Fudge

  ¾ **cup prepared eggnog**
  2 **tablespoons light corn syrup**
  2 **tablespoons butter or margarine**
  2 **cups sugar**
  1 **teaspoon vanilla extract**

1. Butter 8×8-inch pan. Lightly butter inside of heavy, medium saucepan. Combine eggnog, corn syrup, butter and sugar in prepared saucepan. Cook over medium heat, stirring constantly, until sugar dissolves and mixture comes to a boil. Wash down side of pan with pastry brush frequently dipped in hot water to remove sugar crystals. Add candy thermometer. Continue to cook until mixture reaches 238°F (soft-ball stage).

2. Immediately pour into large heatproof bowl. Cool to lukewarm (about 110°F). Add vanilla; beat with heavy-duty electric mixer until thick.

3. Spread in prepared pan. Score fudge into 36 squares. Refrigerate until firm. Cut into squares. Wrap in plastic wrap and top with bows, if desired.

Makes 36 pieces

Bûche de Noël

¾ **cup cake flour**
½ **teaspoon baking powder**
½ **teaspoon salt**
5 **eggs, separated**
1 **cup granulated sugar, divided**
1 **teaspoon vanilla extract**
½ **cup powdered sugar**
1 **cup semisweet chocolate chips**
¾ **cup whipping cream**
1 **tablespoon rum**
  Cocoa Frosting (recipe follows)
  White chocolate curls (optional)
2 **teaspoons unsweetened cocoa powder**

1. Preheat oven to 375°F. Grease 15½×10½-inch jelly-roll pan; line pan with waxed paper. Grease again.

2. Combine flour, baking powder and salt in small bowl.

3. Beat egg yolks and ⅔ cup granulated sugar in small bowl with electric mixer at high speed about 5 minutes or until thick and lemon colored, scraping down side of bowl once. Beat in vanilla; set aside.

4. Beat egg whites until foamy. Gradually beat in remaining ⅓ cup granulated sugar, 1 tablespoon at a time, until stiff peaks form. Fold flour mixture into egg yolk mixture, then fold into egg white mixture.

5. Spread mixture into prepared pan. Bake 12 to 15 minutes until cake springs back when lightly touched with finger. Meanwhile, lightly sift powdered sugar over clean dish towel.

6. Loosen warm cake from edges of pan; invert onto prepared towel. Remove pan; carefully peel off paper. Gently roll up cake in towel from short end, jelly-roll fashion. Let cool completely on wire rack.

7. For chocolate filling, place chocolate chips and cream in heavy 2-quart saucepan. Heat over low heat until chocolate is melted, stirring frequently. Pour into small bowl; stir in rum. Cover and refrigerate about 1½ hours or until filling is spreading consistency, stirring occasionally.

8. Prepare Cocoa Frosting; refrigerate until ready to use. Unroll cake; remove towel. Spread cake with chocolate filling to within ½ inch of edge; reroll cake. Spread Cocoa Frosting over cake roll. Garnish with white chocolate curls, if desired. Sprinkle with cocoa.

Makes 12 servings

Cocoa Frosting

1 **cup whipping cream**
½ **cup powdered sugar, sifted**
2 **tablespoons unsweetened cocoa powder, sifted**
1 **teaspoon vanilla extract**

Beat cream, powdered sugar, cocoa and vanilla with electric mixer at medium speed until soft peaks form. Refrigerate until ready to use.

Makes about 2 cups

Delicate White Chocolate Cake

CAKE

1 package DUNCAN HINES® Moist
   Deluxe White Cake Mix

1 package (4-serving size) vanilla instant
   pudding and pie filling mix

4 egg whites

1 cup water

½ cup CRISCO® Oil or CRISCO®
   PURITAN® Canola Oil

5 ounces finely chopped white chocolate

FILLING

1 cup cherry preserves

8 drops red food coloring (optional)

FROSTING

2 cups whipping cream, chilled

2 tablespoons confectioners sugar
   Maraschino cherries, for garnish

1 ounce white chocolate shavings, for
   garnish (see Tip)

1. Preheat oven to 350°F. Cut waxed paper circles to fit
bottoms of three 9-inch round cake pans. Grease
bottom and sides of pans. Line with waxed paper
circles.

2. For cake, combine cake mix, pudding mix, egg
whites, water and oil in large bowl. Beat at medium
speed with electric mixer for 2 minutes. Fold in

chopped white chocolate. Pour into pans. Bake at 350°F for 18 to 22 minutes. Cool in pans 15 minutes. Invert onto cooling rack. Peel off waxed paper. Cool completely.

3. For filling, combine cherry preserves and food coloring, if desired. Stir to blend color.

4. For frosting, beat whipping cream in large bowl until soft peaks form. Add confectioners sugar gradually. Beat until stiff peaks form.

5. To assemble, place one cake layer on serving plate. Spread ½ cup cherry preserves over cake. Place second cake layer on top. Spread with remaining preserves. Place third cake layer on top. Frost sides and top of cake with whipped cream. Decorate with maraschino cherries and white chocolate shavings. Refrigerate until ready to serve.   *Makes 12 to 16 servings*

Tip: To make white chocolate shavings, use sharp vegetable peeler to slice across square of chocolate.

Rum and Spumoni Layered Torte

1 package (18 to 19 ounces) moist butter
    yellow cake mix
3 eggs
½ cup butter or margarine, softened
⅓ cup plus 2 teaspoons rum, divided
⅓ cup water
1 quart spumoni ice cream, softened
1 cup whipping cream
1 tablespoon powdered sugar
    Chopped mixed candied fruit
    Red and green sugar, for decorating
      (optional)

1. Preheat oven to 375°F. Grease and flour
15½×10½×1-inch jelly-roll pan.

2. Combine cake mix, eggs, butter, ⅓ cup rum and
water in large bowl. Beat with electric mixer on low
speed until moistened. Beat on high speed for 4
minutes. Pour evenly into prepared pan.

3. Bake 20 to 25 minutes until wooden pick inserted in
center comes out clean. Cool in pan 10 minutes. Turn
out of pan onto wire rack; cool completely.

4. Cut cake into three 10×5-inch pieces. Place one cake layer on serving plate. Spread with half the softened ice cream. Cover with second cake layer. Spread with remaining ice cream. Place remaining cake layer on top. Gently push down. Wrap cake in plastic wrap and freeze at least 4 hours.

5. Just before serving, combine cream, powdered sugar and remaining 2 teaspoons rum in small chilled bowl. Beat on high speed with chilled beaters until stiff peaks form. Remove cake from freezer. Spread thin layer of whipped cream mixture over *top* of cake. Place star tip in pastry bag; add remaining whipped cream mixture. Pipe rosettes around outer top edges of cake. Place candied fruit in narrow strip down center of cake. Sprinkle colored sugar over rosettes, if desired. Serve immediately.   *Makes 8 to 10 servings*

Ribbon Cake

CAKE

> 1 package DUNCAN HINES® Moist Deluxe White Cake Mix
> ¼ cup flaked coconut, chopped
> ¾ cup natural pistachio nuts, finely chopped, divided
> Green food coloring
> ¼ cup maraschino cherries, drained, finely chopped
> Red food coloring

FILLING AND FROSTING

> 3¼ cups confectioners sugar
> ½ CRISCO® Stick or ½ cup CRISCO all-vegetable shortening
> ⅓ cup water
> ¼ cup powdered non-dairy creamer
> 1½ teaspoons vanilla extract
> ¼ teaspoon salt
> Green food coloring
> ¾ cup cherry jam
> Whole maraschino cherries with stems, for garnish
> Mint leaves, for garnish

1. Preheat oven to 350°F. Grease and flour three 8-inch square pans.

2. For cake, prepare cake mix following package directions for Basic Recipe. Combine 1¾ cups batter and coconut in small bowl; set aside. Combine 1¾ cups batter, ¼ cup pistachio nuts and 5 drops green food coloring in small bowl; set aside. Combine remaining batter, ¼ cup chopped maraschino cherries and 2 drops red food coloring. Pour batters into separate pans. Bake at 350°F for 18 minutes or until toothpick inserted in center comes out clean. Cool following package directions. Trim edges.

3. For filling and frosting, combine confectioners sugar, shortening, water, non-dairy creamer, vanilla extract, salt and 5 drops green food coloring in large bowl. Beat for 3 minutes at medium speed with electric mixer. Beat for 5 minutes at high speed. Add more confectioners sugar to thicken or water to thin as needed. Add remaining ½ cup pistachio nuts. Stir until blended.

4. To assemble, spread green and white cake layers with cherry jam. Stack layers. Top with remaining pink layer. Frost sides and top of cake. Garnish with whole maraschino cherries and mint leaves.

Makes 12 to 16 servings

Tip: To save time, use DUNCAN HINES® Creamy Homestyle Vanilla Frosting. Tint with several drops green food coloring.

Candy Cane Cake

1 package DUNCAN HINES® Moist
   Deluxe Cake Mix (any flavor)
DECORATOR FROSTING
   5 cups confectioners sugar
   ¾ CRISCO® Stick or ¾ cup CRISCO
      all-vegetable shortening
   ½ cup water
   ⅓ cup non-dairy powdered creamer
   2 teaspoons vanilla extract
   ½ teaspoon salt
      Red food coloring
      Maraschino cherry halves, well drained

1. Preheat oven to 350°F. Grease and flour
13×9×2-inch pan.

2. Prepare, bake and cool cake following package
directions for Basic Recipe. Remove from pan. Freeze
cake for ease in handling.

3. For decorator frosting, combine confectioners
sugar, shortening, water, non-dairy powdered creamer,
vanilla extract and salt in large bowl. Beat at medium
speed with electric mixer for 3 minutes. Beat at high

speed for 5 minutes. Add more confectioners sugar to thicken or water to thin frosting as needed. Reserve 2 cups frosting. Tint remaining frosting with red food coloring.

4. Cut frozen cake and arrange as shown in diagram. Spread white frosting on cake. Mark candy cane stripes in frosting with tip of knife. Place star tip in decorating bag and fill with red frosting. To make candy cane stripes, arrange maraschino cherry halves and pipe red frosting following lines.   *Makes 12 to 16 servings*

Tip: For a quick dessert, serve leftover cake pieces with sugared strawberries and dollops of whipped cream.

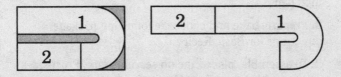

Winter Wonderland Cake

1 **package DUNCAN HINES® Moist Deluxe Cake Mix (any flavor)**
2 **containers (16 ounces each) DUNCAN HINES® Creamy Homestyle Vanilla Frosting**
  Green food coloring
9 **ice cream sugar cones**
½ **cup flaked coconut, finely chopped**
  Marzipan*
  Sliced natural almonds
  Nonpareil decors

1. Preheat oven to 350°F. Grease and flour 13×9×2-inch pan.

2. Prepare, bake and cool cake following package directions for Basic Recipe.

3. To assemble, place cake on serving plate. Frost sides and top with 1 container Vanilla frosting. Tint remaining container of frosting with green food coloring to desired color; set aside. Break off edges of ice cream cones to form various sized trees. Stand cones to form trees. Frost 1 cone with green frosting. Arrange on cake; sprinkle with coconut. Repeat for remaining cones. Form marzipan into bunny shapes. Use almond slices for ears and nonpareil decors for eyes and noses. Arrange as desired. Sprinkle remaining coconut on cake.   *Makes 12 to 16 servings*

*Marzipan, a cooked mixture of finely ground almonds, sugar and egg whites, is very sweet and pliable. It is available in most supermarkets packaged in cans or in plastic-wrapped logs.

Cherry Christmas Wreaths

1 **package DUNCAN HINES® Moist
     Deluxe Devil's Food Cake Mix**
2 **containers (16 ounces each) DUNCAN
     HINES® Creamy Homestyle Cream
     Cheese Frosting, divided**
  Green food coloring
1 **can (20 ounces) lite cherry pie filling**
½ **teaspoon ground cinnamon**
¼ **teaspoon almond extract**

1. Preheat oven to 350°F. Grease and flour 10-inch tube pan.

2. Prepare, bake and cool cake following package directions for Basic Recipe.

3. Split cake in half horizontally. Reserve 1 cup Cream Cheese frosting. Spread remaining frosting on sides and tops of both cakes. Tint reserved frosting with green food coloring. Place star tip in decorating bag; fill with green frosting. Pipe decorative edge around top (including center top edge) and bottom of each cake.

4. Combine cherry pie filling, cinnamon and almond extract in medium bowl. Spoon half the cherry mixture on top of each cake between green frosting rings. Refrigerate until ready to serve.

Makes 16 to 20 servings

Note: Recipe makes two Cherry Christmas Wreaths.

Tip: For ease of preparation, freeze split cake layers before frosting and decorating.

Fudgey Valentine Cake

⅔ cup butter or margarine, softened
1¾ cups sugar
2 eggs
1 teaspoon vanilla extract
1¾ cups all-purpose flour
¾ cup HERSHEY®'S Cocoa or
   HERSHEY®'S European Style Cocoa
1½ teaspoons baking soda
1 teaspoon salt
1½ cups dairy sour cream
   Pink Buttercream Frosting (recipe follows)
   Maraschino cherries (optional)

Heat oven to 350°F. Grease and flour two 9-inch heart-shaped pans.* In large bowl, beat butter and sugar until creamy. Add eggs and vanilla; beat well. Stir together flour, cocoa, baking soda and salt; add to butter mixture alternately with sour cream, beating well after each addition. Beat 3 minutes on medium speed of electric mixer. Pour batter evenly into prepared pans. Bake 35 to 40 minutes or until wooden pick inserted in center comes out clean. Cool 10 minutes; remove from pans to wire racks. Cool completely. Prepare Pink Buttercream Frosting; spread between layers and over top and sides of cake. Garnish with cherries, if desired.   *Makes 10 to 12 servings*

*One 8-inch square baking pan and one 8-inch round baking pan (each must be 2 inches deep) may be substituted for heart-shaped pans. Prepare, bake and cool cake as directed above. Cut round layer in half, forming two half circles; place cut edge of each half circle against sides of square layer to form heart.

Pink Buttercream Frosting

½ cup (1 stick) butter or margarine,
   softened
4¼ cups powdered sugar
4 tablespoons milk
2 teaspoons vanilla extract
¼ teaspoon red food color

In medium bowl, beat butter until creamy. Gradually
add powdered sugar alternately with combined milk
and vanilla, beating well after each addition until
smooth and of spreading consistency. Stir in food
color. Add additional milk, 1 teaspoon at a time, if
needed.

Autumn Gold Pumpkin Cake

CAKE

- 1 package DUNCAN HINES® Moist Deluxe Butter Recipe Golden Cake Mix
- 3 eggs
- 1 cup water
- 1 cup solid pack pumpkin
- 1 teaspoon ground cinnamon
- ¼ teaspoon ground ginger
- ¼ teaspoon ground nutmeg
- 1 cup chopped walnuts

FROSTING

- 1 container (16 ounces) DUNCAN HINES® Creamy Homestyle Vanilla Frosting
- ½ teaspoon ground cinnamon
- ¼ cup coarsely chopped walnuts, for garnish

1. Preheat oven to 375°F. Grease and flour two 8-inch round cake pans.

2. For cake, combine cake mix, eggs, water, pumpkin, 1 teaspoon cinnamon, ginger and nutmeg in large bowl. Beat at medium speed with electric mixer for 4 minutes. Stir in 1 cup walnuts. Pour batter into pans. Bake at 375°F for 30 to 35 minutes or until toothpick inserted in center comes out clean. Cool following package directions.

3. For frosting, combine Vanilla frosting and
½ teaspoon cinnamon. Stir until blended. Fill and frost
cake. Garnish with ¼ cup walnuts.

Makes 12 to 16 servings

Tip: You may also bake this cake in a greased and
floured 13×9×2-inch pan at 375°F for 30 minutes or
until toothpick inserted in center comes out clean.

Pumpkin Crunch Cake

    1 package (18.25 ounces) yellow cake
          mix, *divided*
    2 eggs
   1⅔ cups LIBBY'S® Pumpkin Pie Mix
    2 teaspoons pumpkin pie spice
    ⅓ cup flake coconut
    ¼ cup chopped nuts
    3 tablespoons butter or margarine,
          softened

COMBINE *3 cups* cake mix, eggs, pumpkin pie mix
and pumpkin pie spice in large mixer bowl. Beat on
low speed until moistened. Beat on medium speed for
2 minutes. Pour into greased 13×9-inch baking pan.

COMBINE *remaining* cake mix, coconut and nuts in
small bowl; cut in butter with pastry blender or two
knives until mixture is crumbly. Sprinkle over batter.

BAKE in preheated 350°F. oven for 30 to 35 minutes or
until wooden pick inserted in center comes out clean.
Cool in pan on wire rack.   *Makes 20 servings*

Pumpkin Pie Crunch

1 can (16 ounces) solid pack pumpkin
1 can (12 ounces) evaporated milk
3 eggs
1½ cups sugar
4 teaspoons pumpkin pie spice
½ teaspoon salt
1 package DUNCAN HINES® Moist
    Deluxe Yellow Cake Mix
1 cup chopped pecans
1 cup butter or margarine, melted
    Whipped topping

1. Preheat oven to 350°F. Grease bottom of 13×9×2-inch pan.

2. Combine pumpkin, evaporated milk, eggs, sugar, pumpkin pie spice and salt in large bowl. Pour into pan. Sprinkle cake mix evenly over pumpkin mixture. Top with pecans. Drizzle with melted butter. Bake at 350°F for 50 to 55 minutes or until golden. Cool completely. Cut into squares. Serve with whipped topping. Refrigerate leftovers.

Makes 16 to 20 servings

Tip: For a richer flavor, try using DUNCAN HINES® Moist Deluxe Butter Recipe Golden Cake Mix.

Poached Pears in Cranberry Syrup

- 1 **quart (4 cups) cranberry juice cocktail**
- 1 **cup KARO® Light Corn Syrup**
- 8 **slices (¼ inch thick) unpeeled fresh ginger**
- 2 **cinnamon sticks (2 to 3 inches)**
- 8 **slightly underripe pears**

1. In heavy 4-quart saucepan combine cranberry juice, corn syrup, ginger and cinnamon sticks; bring to boil over medium-high heat.

2. Peel pears, leaving stems attached. Add to cranberry liquid; cover. Reduce heat and simmer 15 to 20 minutes or until pears are tender.

3. With slotted spoon transfer pears to shallow serving dish. Remove ginger slices and cinnamon sticks.

4. Discard all but 2 cups syrup in saucepan. Bring to boil; boil 10 to 12 minutes or until syrup thickens slightly. Spoon sauce over pears.

Makes 8 servings

Old-Fashioned Gingerbread

2 tablespoons margarine, melted and cooled
⅓ cup firmly packed brown sugar
¼ cup cholesterol free egg substitute
¼ cup buttermilk
2 cups all-purpose flour
1½ teaspoons baking soda
1½ teaspoons ground ginger
1 teaspoon ground cinnamon
½ teaspoon salt
1 tablespoon instant decaffeinated coffee granules
1 cup hot water
½ cup molasses
¼ cup honey
1 jar (2½ ounces) puréed prunes
   Reduced fat nondairy whipped topping (optional)

1. Preheat oven to 350°F. Spray 9-inch square or 11×7-inch baking pan with nonstick cooking spray.

2. Combine margarine, brown sugar, egg substitute and buttermilk in medium bowl; set aside. Combine flour, baking soda, ginger, cinnamon and salt in large bowl; set aside. Dissolve coffee granules in hot water in small bowl. Stir in molasses, honey and puréed prunes.

3. Add flour mixture alternately with coffee mixture to margarine mixture. Batter will be lumpy. *Do not overmix.*

4. Pour batter into prepared pan. Bake 40 to 45 minutes until wooden pick inserted in center comes out clean. Cool in pan on wire rack. Before serving, top with whipped topping, if desired.

Makes 8 servings

Apple and Cream Cheese Bake

1 package (8 ounces) PHILADELPHIA
   BRAND® FREE® Fat Free Cream
   Cheese, softened
½ cup granulated sugar
1 egg
2 tablespoons flour
1 teaspoon ground cinnamon
½ teaspoon vanilla
4 cups chopped peeled apples
⅓ cup flour
½ cup firmly packed brown sugar
2 tablespoons reduced-fat tablespread,
   cold

BEAT cream cheese with electric mixer on medium
speed until smooth. Add granulated sugar, egg, 2
tablespoons flour, cinnamon and vanilla, mixing until
blended. Stir in apples. Pour into 8-inch square baking
dish that has been sprayed with nonstick cooking
spray.

MIX ⅓ cup flour and brown sugar; cut in tablespread
until mixture resembles coarse crumbs. Sprinkle over
apple mixture.

BAKE at 350°F for 40 minutes. Serve warm. Garnish
with apple slices, if desired.   *Makes 9 servings*

Thanksgiving Cranberry Cobbler

2 cans (16 ounces each) sliced peaches in light syrup, drained
1 can (16 ounces) whole berry cranberry sauce
1 package DUNCAN HINES® Cinnamon Muffin Mix
½ cup chopped pecans
⅓ cup butter or margarine, melted
Whipped topping or ice cream

1. Preheat oven to 350°F.

2. Cut peach slices in half lengthwise. Combine peach slices and cranberry sauce in ungreased 9-inch square pan. Knead swirl packet from Mix for 10 seconds. Cut off one end of packet. Squeeze contents evenly over fruit.

3. Combine muffin mix, topping packet from Mix and pecans in large bowl. Add melted butter. Stir until thoroughly blended. (Mixture will be crumbly.) Sprinkle crumbs over fruit. Bake at 350°F for 40 to 45 minutes or until lightly browned and bubbly. Serve warm with whipped topping or ice cream.

Makes 9 servings

Tip: Store shelled pecans in the refrigerator for up to 3 months or in the freezer for up to 6 months.

Cranberry-Apple Strudel

Butter-flavored nonstick cooking spray
1 tablespoon margarine
1 tablespoon firmly packed light brown sugar
2 medium Golden Delicious apples, cored, peeled and diced
¼ cup raisins
1 can (16 ounces) whole-berry cranberry sauce
6 sheets phyllo dough
3 tablespoons graham cracker crumbs, divided
¼ cup toasted almonds, chopped

1. Preheat oven to 375°F. Spray cookie sheet with butter-flavored nonstick cooking spray. Melt margarine in large saucepan over medium heat. Add brown sugar; bring to a boil. Add apples and raisins; cook 10 minutes or until apples can be easily pierced with fork. Remove from heat. Add cranberry sauce; mix well. Set aside.

2. Place 1 sheet of phyllo on piece of parchment paper with narrow side farthest away. Spray phyllo with cooking spray; sprinkle ½ tablespoon graham cracker crumbs on phyllo. Overlap second sheet of phyllo over first sheet about 1 inch down from top. Spray with cooking spray; sprinkle with ½ tablespoon crumbs.

Continue overlapping with remaining phyllo and crumbs, spraying with cooking spray between each layer.

3. Spoon cooled cranberry mixture into center of phyllo. Sprinkle chopped almonds over mixture. Fold bottom and sides of phyllo to cover mixture, forming an envelope. With floured hands, roll filled phyllo, jelly-roll fashion, to form strudel. Place strudel on prepared cookie sheet. Spray top with cooking spray. Make 8 diagonal cuts across top of strudel. Bake 12 to 15 minutes or until lightly browned.

4. Cool on wire rack 30 minutes. Cut crosswise into 8 pieces.   *Makes 8 servings*

Cranberry Apple Crisp

⅓ to ½ cup sugar
3 tablespoons ARGO® or KINGSFORD'S®
    Corn Starch
1 teaspoon cinnamon
½ teaspoon nutmeg
5 to 6 cups cubed peeled tart apples
1 cup fresh or frozen cranberries
½ cup KARO® Light Corn Syrup
1 teaspoon grated orange peel

TOPPING
½ cup chopped walnuts or uncooked oats
⅓ cup packed brown sugar
¼ cup flour
¼ cup (½ stick) MAZOLA® Margarine or
    butter

1. Preheat oven to 350°F. In large bowl combine sugar, corn starch, cinnamon and nutmeg. Add apples, cranberries, corn syrup and orange peel; toss to mix well. Spoon into 8-inch square baking dish.

2. For Topping, combine nuts, brown sugar and flour. With pastry blender or 2 knives, cut in margarine until mixture resembles very coarse crumbs. Sprinkle over cranberry mixture.

3. Bake 50 minutes or until apples are tender and juices that bubble up in center are shiny and clear. Cool slightly; serve warm. *Makes 6 to 8 servings*

Shamrock Parfaits

1   envelope unflavored gelatin
½   cup cold water
¾   cup sugar
½   cup HERSHEY¡S Cocoa
1¼   cups evaporated skim milk
1   teaspoon vanilla extract
2   cups frozen whipped topping, thawed,
       divided
⅛   teaspoon mint extract
6   to 7 drops green food color

In medium saucepan, sprinkle gelatin over water; let
stand 2 minutes to soften. Cook over low heat about
3 minutes or until gelatin is completely dissolved,
stirring constantly. In small bowl, stir together sugar
and cocoa; gradually add to gelatin mixture, stirring
with whisk until well blended. Continue cooking over
low heat until sugar is dissolved, stirring constantly.
Remove from heat. Stir in evaporated milk and vanilla.
Pour mixture into large bowl. Refrigerate about 20
minutes or until mixture mounds slightly when
dropped from spoon, stirring occasionally. Fold ½ cup
whipped topping into chocolate mixture. Divide about
half of mixture evenly among eight parfait or wine
glasses. Stir mint extract and food color into remaining
1½ cups topping; divide evenly among glasses. Spoon
remaining chocolate mixture over topping in each
glass. Garnish as desired. Serve immediately or
refrigerate until serving time. Cover; refrigerate
leftover parfaits.   *Makes about 8 servings*

Perfect

PIES

Apple Almond Pie

- ¾ cup sugar, divided
- ¼ cup ARGO® or KINGSFORD'S® Corn Starch
- 3 eggs
- ½ cup (1 stick) MAZOLA® Margarine, melted
- ½ cup KARO® Light or Dark Corn Syrup
- ¼ teaspoon almond extract
- 2 cups peeled, chopped apples (about 2 large)
- 1 cup sliced or slivered almonds, toasted Easy-As-Pie Crust (page 268)
- 1 apple, peeled and thinly sliced (optional)
  Sliced almonds, toasted (optional)

1. Preheat oven to 375°F. Reserve 2 tablespoons sugar.

2. In medium bowl combine remaining sugar and corn starch. Beat in eggs until well blended. Stir in margarine, corn syrup and almond extract. Mix in chopped apples and almonds. Pour into pie crust.

3. If desired, garnish with apple slices arranged in a circle around edge of pie; fill center with additional toasted almonds. Sprinkle reserved sugar over top.

4. Bake 50 minutes or until puffed and set. Cool on wire rack.   *Makes 8 servings*

Country Apple Rhubarb Pie

CRUST
> **9-inch Classic CRISCO® Double Crust (page 250)**

FILLING
- 9 cups sliced, peeled Granny Smith apples (about 3 pounds or 6 large apples)
- 1½ cups chopped (about ½ inch) fresh rhubarb, peeled if tough
- ¾ cup granulated sugar
- ½ cup firmly packed light brown sugar
- 2 tablespoons all-purpose flour
- 1 tablespoon cornstarch
- 1 teaspoon ground cinnamon
- ¼ teaspoon freshly grated nutmeg

GLAZE
- 1 egg, beaten
- 1 tablespoon water
- 1 tablespoon granulated sugar
- 1 teaspoon ground pecans or walnuts
- ⅛ teaspoon ground cinnamon

1. *For crust,* **prepare** as directed. **Roll** and press bottom crust into 9- or 9½-inch deep-dish glass pie plate. *Do not bake.* **Heat** oven to 425°F.

2. *For filling,* combine apples and rhubarb in large bowl. **Combine** ¾ cup granulated sugar, brown sugar, flour, cornstarch, 1 teaspoon cinnamon and nutmeg in medium bowl. **Sprinkle** over fruit. **Toss** to coat. **Spoon** into unbaked pie crust. **Moisten** pastry edge with water. **Cover** pie with lattice top, cutting strips 1 inch wide. **Flute** edge high.

3. *For glaze,* combine egg and water in small bowl. **Brush** over crust. **Combine** remaining glaze ingredients in small bowl. **Sprinkle** over crust.

4. Bake at 425°F for 20 minutes. *Reduce oven temperature to 350°F.* **Bake** 30 to 40 minutes or until filling in center is bubbly and crust is golden brown. **Place** sheet of foil or baking sheet under pie if it starts to bubble over. **Cool** to room temperature.

Makes one 9- or 9½-inch deep-dish pie (8 servings)

Apples 'n' Honey Nut Tart

1¼ cups all-purpose flour
⅓ cup wheat germ
⅓ cup packed brown sugar
½ teaspoon salt
¾ teaspoon grated orange peel, divided
½ cup cold butter, cut into pieces
1 egg, beaten
1 cup coarsely chopped pecans
⅓ cup golden raisins
2½ pounds apples
8 tablespoons honey, divided
2 tablespoons butter, melted
½ teaspoon ground cinnamon
⅓ cup orange marmalade
⅔ cup whipping cream, chilled

1. Combine flour, wheat germ, brown sugar, salt and ½ teaspoon grated orange peel in large bowl. Cut in ½ cup cold butter with pastry blender or 2 knives until mixture forms pea-sized pieces. Add egg; stir until well blended. Press firmly onto bottom and up side of 9-inch tart pan with removable bottom. Freeze until very firm, about 30 minutes.

2. Preheat oven to 350°F.

3. Combine pecans and raisins in small bowl. Sprinkle on bottom of chilled crust.

4. Peel apples. Remove cores; discard. Cut apples into ¼-inch-thick slices.

5. Combine 6 tablespoons honey, 2 tablespoons melted butter, remaining ¼ teaspoon orange peel, cinnamon and apple slices in large bowl; stir to coat apples. Arrange apple slices in circular pattern on top of pecans and raisins.

6. For center slice, place peeled apple, with stem facing away from you, on cutting board. Cut a ¼-inch-thick slice from center of apple. Place in center of tart.

7. Drizzle any honey mixture left in bowl over apples. Bake 50 to 55 minutes until apples are tender.

8. Place marmalade in small saucepan. Heat over medium heat until warm, stirring occasionally. Brush over apples. Cool; remove side of tart pan.

9. Pour cream and remaining 2 tablespoons honey into chilled bowl and beat with electric mixer at high speed until soft peaks form. Serve with tart.

Makes 8 to 10 servings

Autumn Pear Tart

Reduced Fat Pastry (recipe follows)
3 to 4 tablespoons sugar
2 tablespoons cornstarch
3 to 4 large pears, cut into halves, cored,
    peeled and sliced
1 tablespoon lemon juice
   Ground cinnamon (optional)
   Ground nutmeg (optional)
¼ cup apple jelly, apricot spreadable fruit
    or honey, warmed

1. Preheat oven to 425°F. Roll out pastry on floured surface to ⅛-inch thickness. Ease pastry into 9-inch tart pan; trim edge. Pierce bottom of pastry with tines of fork; bake 15 to 20 minutes until pastry begins to brown. Cool on wire rack.

2. Combine sugar and cornstarch in small bowl; mix well. Sprinkle pears with lemon juice; toss with sugar mixture. Arrange sliced pears on pastry. Sprinkle lightly with cinnamon and nutmeg, if desired.

3. Bake 20 to 30 minutes until pears are tender and crust is browned. Cool on wire rack. Brush pears with jelly. Remove side of pan; place tart on serving plate.

Makes 8 servings

Reduced Fat Pastry

1⅓ cups cake flour
2 tablespoons sugar
¼ teaspoon salt
¼ cup vegetable shortening
4 to 5 tablespoons ice water

Combine flour, sugar and salt in small bowl. Cut in shortening with pastry blender or two knives until mixture forms coarse crumbs. Mix in ice water, 1 tablespoon at a time, until mixture comes together and forms a soft dough. Wrap in plastic wrap. Refrigerate 30 minutes before using.

Makes pastry for one 9-inch tart

Ginger & Pear Tart

30 **gingersnap cookies**
½ **cup chopped pecans**
⅓ **cup butter, melted**
1 **cup sour cream**
¾ **cup half-and-half**
1 **package (4-serving size) vanilla instant pudding mix**
2 **tablespoons apricot brandy**
4 **ripe pears***
⅓ **cup packed dark brown sugar**
½ **teaspoon ground ginger**

*Or, substitute 1 (16-ounce) can pear halves, drained and thinly sliced, for fresh pears.

1. Preheat oven to 350°F.

2. Place cookies and pecans in food processor or blender container; process with on/off pulses until finely crushed.

3. Combine crumb mixture and butter in medium bowl. Press firmly onto bottom and up side of 10-inch quiche dish or 9-inch pie plate. Bake 7 minutes; cool completely on wire rack.

4. Combine sour cream and half-and-half in large bowl. Beat until smooth. Whisk in pudding mix. Add apricot brandy. Beat until smooth.

5. Pour into prepared crust. Cover; refrigerate several hours or overnight.

6. Just before serving, preheat broiler. Peel pears. Cut pears in half lengthwise. Remove cores and seeds; discard. Thinly slice pears. Arrange pear slices in overlapping circles on top of pudding mixture.

7. Combine brown sugar and ginger in small bowl. Sprinkle evenly over pears. Broil 4 to 6 minutes until sugar is melted and bubbly. Watch carefully so sugar does not burn. Serve immediately.

Makes 6 to 8 servings

Luscious Cranberry and Blueberry Pie

CRUST

   1   unbaked 9-inch Classic CRISCO®
        Double Crust (page 250)
   ½   teaspoon ground mace

FILLING

   1   can (16 ounces) whole berry cranberry
        sauce
   ⅓   cup packed brown sugar
   ¼   cup granulated sugar
   2   tablespoons all-purpose flour
   2   tablespoons cornstarch
   2   tablespoons orange juice
   ½   teaspoon dried grated orange peel
   ⅛   teaspoon salt
   2   cups fresh or frozen blueberries
   2   tablespoons butter or margarine

GLAZE

   1   egg, beaten

1. *For Crust,* **prepare** 9-inch Classic CRISCO® Double Crust, adding mace to flour mixture. **Roll** and press bottom crust into 9-inch pie plate. *Do not bake.* **Reserve** dough scraps for decorations, if desired. **Heat** oven to 425°F.

2. *For Filling,* **combine** cranberry sauce, brown sugar, granulated sugar, flour, cornstarch, orange juice, orange peel and salt in large bowl. **Stir** in blueberries. **Spoon** into unbaked pie crust; dot with butter. **Moisten** pastry edge with water.

3. Roll out top crust; lift crust onto filled pie. **Trim** ½ inch beyond edge of pie plate. **Fold** top edge under bottom crust; flute. **Cut** blossom-shaped holes in top crust to allow steam to escape.

4. Cut flowers or other shapes from reserved dough. **Place** on top of pie. *For Glaze,* **brush** with egg. **Bake** at 425°F for 40 minutes or until filling in center is bubbly and crust is golden brown. **Cover** edge with foil during last 10 minutes to prevent overbrowning. **Cool** to room temperature before serving.

Makes one 9-inch pie

Classic Cherry Pie

CRUST

1 unbaked 9-inch Classic CRISCO®
Double Crust (page 250)

FILLING

3 pounds pitted red tart cherries frozen
with sugar, thawed*

⅓ cup granulated sugar

⅓ cup firmly packed brown sugar

¼ cup cornstarch

½ teaspoon ground cinnamon

1½ cups reserved cherry juice*

1½ tablespoons CRISCO® Stick or
BUTTER FLAVOR** CRISCO®
all-vegetable shortening

1 tablespoon vanilla

1 teaspoon almond extract

GLAZE

Milk

Additional granulated sugar

*Use 2 cans (1 pound each) red tart cherries packed in water in place
of frozen. Reduce cherry liquid to 1 cup.

**Butter Flavor Crisco is artificially flavored.

1. *For Crust,* prepare 9-inch Classic CRISCO® Double
Crust. **Roll** and press into 9-inch pie plate. *Do not
bake.* **Heat** oven to 425°F.

2. *For Filling,* drain cherries in large strainer over bowl, reserving 1½ cups juice. **Combine** sugars, cornstarch and cinnamon in large saucepan. **Stir** in reserved 1½ cups cherry juice. **Cook** and stir on medium heat until mixture is thick and bubbly. **Boil** and stir 1 minute. **Add** cherries and cook 1 minute or until mixture comes to a boil. **Remove** from heat. **Stir** in shortening, vanilla and almond extract. **Spoon** into unbaked pie crust. **Moisten** pastry edge with water.

3. Roll out top crust; lift crust onto filled pie. **Trim** ½ inch beyond edge of pie plate. **Fold** top edge under bottom crust; flute with fingers or fork. **Cut** slits in top crust to allow steam to escape.

4. *For Glaze,* brush top crust with milk. **Sprinkle** with additional granulated sugar. **Bake** at 425°F for 15 minutes. *Reduce oven temperature to 350°F.*

5. Bake 25 minutes or until filling in center is bubbly and crust is golden brown. **Cool** until barely warm or to room temperature before serving.

Makes one 9-inch pie

LIBBY'S® Famous Pumpkin Pie

- 1 *unbaked* 9-inch (4-cup volume) deep-dish pie shell
- ¾ cup granulated sugar
- ½ teaspoon salt
- 1 teaspoon ground cinnamon
- ½ teaspoon ground ginger
- ¼ teaspoon ground cloves
- 2 eggs
- 1¾ cups (15-ounce can) LIBBY'S® Solid Pack Pumpkin
- 1½ cups (12 fluid-ounce can) CARNATION® Evaporated Milk

COMBINE sugar, salt, cinnamon, ginger and cloves in small bowl. Beat eggs lightly in large bowl. Stir in pumpkin and sugar-spice mixture. Gradually stir in evaporated milk. Pour into pie shell.

BAKE in preheated 425°F. oven for 15 minutes. *Reduce temperature to 350°F.;* bake for 40 to 50 minutes or until knife inserted near center comes out clean. Cool on wire rack for 2 hours. Serve immediately or chill (do not freeze).

Makes 8 servings

For 2 shallow pies, substitute two 9-inch (2-cup volume) pie shells. Bake in preheated 425°F. oven for 15 minutes. *Reduce temperature to 350°F.;* bake for 20 to 30 minutes or until pies test done.

For lower fat/calorie pie, substitute CARNATION® Evaporated Lowfat or Evaporated Skimmed Milk.

Quick & Easy Chocolate Chip Cherry Pie

1 can (21 ounces) cherry pie filling
1 tablespoon cornstarch
1 extra serving-size packaged graham
     cracker crumb crust (9 ounces)
1 package (8 ounces) cream cheese,
     softened
¼ cup sugar
2 eggs
½ teaspoon vanilla extract
½ teaspoon almond extract
½ cup HERSHEY₅S Semi-Sweet
     Chocolate Chips or HERSHEY₅S
     MINI CHIPS₀ Semi-Sweet Chocolate

Heat oven to 350°F. In medium bowl, stir together pie
filling and cornstarch until blended; pour into crust. In
small bowl, beat cream cheese, sugar, eggs, vanilla and
almond extract until blended; pour over pie filling.
Sprinkle chocolate chips evenly over top. Bake 35 to 40
minutes or until almost set in center. Cool completely
on wire rack. Cover; refrigerate until firm. Refrigerate
leftover pie.   *Makes 8 to 10 servings*

Classic CRISCO® Crust

8-, 9- or 10-INCH SINGLE CRUST
- 1⅓ cups all-purpose flour
- ½ teaspoon salt
- ½ CRISCO® Stick or ½ cup CRISCO all-vegetable shortening
- 3 tablespoons cold water

8- or 9-INCH DOUBLE CRUST
- 2 cups all-purpose flour
- 1 teaspoon salt
- ¾ CRISCO Stick or ¾ cup CRISCO all-vegetable shortening
- 5 tablespoons cold water

10-INCH DOUBLE CRUST
- 2⅔ cups all-purpose flour
- 1 teaspoon salt
- 1 CRISCO Stick or 1 cup CRISCO all-vegetable shortening
- 7 to 8 tablespoons cold water

1. Spoon flour into measuring cup and level. **Combine** flour and salt in medium bowl.

2. Cut in shortening using pastry blender (or 2 knives) until all flour is blended to form pea-size chunks.

3. Sprinkle with water, 1 tablespoon at a time. **Toss** lightly with fork until dough forms a ball.

For Single Crust Pies

1. Press dough between hands to form 5- to 6-inch "pancake." **Flour** rolling surface and rolling pin lightly. **Roll** dough into circle.

2. Trim 1 inch larger than upside-down pie plate. **Loosen** dough carefully.

3. Fold dough into quarters. **Unfold** and **press** into pie plate. **Fold** edge under. **Flute.**

For Baked Pie Crusts

1. For recipes using baked pie crust, **heat** oven to 425°F. **Prick** bottom and side thoroughly with fork (50 times) to prevent shrinkage.

2. Bake at 425°F for 10 to 15 minutes or until lightly browned.

For Unbaked Pie Crusts

1. For recipes using unbaked pie crust, **follow** baking directions given in each recipe.

For Double Crust Pies

1. Divide dough in half. **Roll** each half separately. **Transfer** bottom crust to pie plate. **Trim** edge even with pie plate.

2. Add desired filling to unbaked pie crust. **Moisten** pastry edge with water. **Lift** top crust onto filled pie. **Trim** ½ inch beyond edge of pie plate. **Fold** top edge under bottom crust. **Flute. Cut** slits in top crust to allow steam to escape. **Bake** according to specific recipe directions.

Summer Fruit Pie

CRUST

>9-inch Classic CRISCO® Double Crust
>(page 250)

CREAM CHEESE LAYER

- 4 ounces (half of 8-ounce package) cream cheese, softened
- 1 egg
- 2 tablespoons sugar
- ¼ cup chopped natural or blanched almonds
- 1 teaspoon all-purpose flour

FRUIT LAYER

- ¾ cup sugar
- ¼ cup all-purpose flour
- 1 can (16 or 17 ounces) pitted Royal Anne or dark sweet cherries packed in heavy or extra heavy syrup, rinsed and drained
- 2½ cups sliced, peeled freestone peaches (about 1¼ pounds or 5 medium peaches)
- 1 teaspoon fresh lemon juice
- ¼ cup almond-flavored liqueur

1. *For crust,* **prepare** as directed. **Roll** and **press** bottom crust into 9-inch glass pie plate. *Do not bake.* **Heat** oven to 400°F.

2. *For cream cheese layer,* **combine** cream cheese, egg and 2 tablespoons sugar in small bowl. **Mix** with spoon until smooth. **Stir** in nuts. **Dust** bottom of unbaked pie crust with 1 teaspoon flour. **Spread** cheese mixture over flour.

3. *For fruit layer,* **combine** ¾ cup sugar and ¼ cup flour in small bowl. **Sprinkle** about one-third of mixture over cheese layer.

4. Combine cherries, peaches and lemon juice in large bowl. **Sprinkle** remaining sugar mixture over fruit mixture. **Toss** to coat. **Stir** in almond-flavored liqueur. **Spoon** over sugar mixture in pie crust. **Moisten** pastry edge with water.

5. Cover pie with lattice top, cutting strips 1 inch wide. **Flute** edge and press with fork.

6. Bake at 400°F for 45 to 50 minutes or until filling in center is bubbly and crust is golden brown. **Cool** to room temperature before serving. **Refrigerate** leftovers.

Makes one 9-inch pie (8 servings)

Secret Chocolate Strawberry Pie

3 cups sliced fresh strawberries (about
2½ pints), divided
1 cup sugar
2 teaspoons cornstarch
1 package (3 ounces) strawberry-flavored
gelatin
1 tablespoon butter or margarine
1 tablespoon lemon juice
¼ cup HERSHEY¿S Semi-Sweet
Chocolate Chips
4 tablespoons whipping cream, divided
1 baked 9-inch pie crust, cooled
1 package (3 ounces) cream cheese,
softened
Sweetened whipped cream (optional)
Whole strawberries (optional)

Reserve 2 cups sliced strawberries. Mash remaining
1 cup sliced strawberries; add enough water to make
2 cups. In medium saucepan, stir together sugar and
cornstarch; stir in mashed strawberries. Cook over
medium heat until mixture comes to a boil, stirring
constantly; cook 2 minutes, stirring constantly.
Remove from heat. Add gelatin, butter and lemon
juice; stir until gelatin is dissolved. Strain mixture;
discard seeds. Refrigerate until partially set.

Meanwhile, in small microwave-safe bowl, place chocolate chips and 3 tablespoons whipping cream. Microwave at HIGH (100%) 1 minute; stir. If necessary, microwave at HIGH an additional 15 seconds at a time, stirring after each heating, just until chips are melted when stirred. Spread chocolate mixture onto bottom of prepared crust; refrigerate 30 minutes or until firm. In small bowl, beat cream cheese and remaining 1 tablespoon whipping cream until smooth; spread over chocolate layer. Refrigerate filled crust while gelatin mixture is cooling. When gelatin mixture is partially set, fold in reserved sliced strawberries; spoon mixture over cream cheese layer. Cover; refrigerate several hours or until firm. Just before serving, garnish with sweetened whipped cream and whole strawberries, if desired. Refrigerate leftover pie.

Makes 8 servings

Amaretto Coconut Cream Pie

¼ cup flaked coconut
1 container (8 ounces) thawed nondairy whipped topping, divided
1 container (8 ounces) coconut cream-flavored or vanilla-flavored yogurt
¼ cup amaretto liqueur
1 package (4-serving size) instant coconut pudding and pie filling mix
1 prepared (9-inch) graham cracker pie crust
Fresh strawberries and mint leaves (optional)

1. Preheat oven to 350°F. To toast coconut, place coconut on baking sheet. Bake 4 to 5 minutes until golden brown, stirring frequently. Cool completely.

2. Place 2 cups whipped topping, yogurt and amaretto in large bowl. Add pudding mix. Beat with wire whisk or electric mixer on low speed, 1 to 2 minutes until thickened.

3. Pour pudding mixture into crust; spread remaining whipped topping over filling. Sprinkle with toasted coconut. Garnish with fresh strawberries and mint leaves, if desired. Refrigerate.   *Makes 8 servings*

Grasshopper Pie

- 2 cups graham cracker crumbs
- 4 tablespoons unsweetened cocoa powder
- ¼ cup margarine, melted
- 8 ounces nonfat cream cheese
- 1 cup 1% low-fat milk
- 2 tablespoons green crème de menthe liqueur
- 2 tablespoons white crème de cacao liqueur
- 1½ teaspoons vanilla extract
- 1 container (4 ounces) frozen nondairy whipped topping, thawed

1. Spray 9-inch pie plate with nonstick cooking spray. Combine cracker crumbs, cocoa and margarine in medium bowl. Press onto bottom and up side of prepared pie plate. Refrigerate.

2. Beat cream cheese in large bowl with electric mixer until fluffy. Gradually beat in milk until smooth. Stir in both liqueurs and vanilla. Fold in whipped topping. Chill 20 minutes or until cool but not set. Pour into chilled crust. Freeze 4 hours or until set.

Makes 8 servings

Fresh Lemon Meringue Pie

1½ cups sugar
¼   cup plus 2 tablespoons cornstarch
½   teaspoon salt
½   cup cold water
½   cup fresh squeezed lemon juice
3   egg yolks, well beaten
2   tablespoons butter or margarine
1½ cups boiling water
    Grated peel of ½ SUNKIST® Lemon
2   drops yellow food coloring (optional)
1   (9-inch) baked pie crust
    Three-Egg Meringue (recipe follows)

In large saucepan, combine sugar, cornstarch and salt.
Gradually blend in cold water and lemon juice. Stir in
egg yolks. Add butter and boiling water. Bring to a boil
over medium-high heat, stirring constantly. Reduce
heat to medium and boil 1 minute. Remove from heat;
stir in lemon peel and food coloring. Pour into baked
pie crust. Top with Three-Egg Meringue, sealing well at
edges. Bake at 350°F 12 to 15 minutes. Cool 2 hours
before serving.   *Makes 6 servings*

Three-Egg Meringue

3   egg whites
¼   teaspoon cream of tartar
6   tablespoons sugar

In large bowl, with electric mixer, beat egg whites with
cream of tartar until foamy. Gradually add sugar and
beat until stiff peaks form.

Lemon Dream Pie

1 **package (8 ounces) cream cheese,
   softened**
¾ **cup sugar, divided**
3 **eggs, divided
   Easy-As-Pie Crust (page 268)**
¾ **cup KARO® Light Corn Syrup**
⅓ **cup lemon juice**
2 **tablespoons MAZOLA® Margarine,
   melted**
1 **tablespoon ARGO® or KINGSFORD'S®
   Corn Starch**
2 **teaspoons grated lemon peel
   Whipped cream, lemon peel and pastry
   cut-outs**

1. Preheat oven to 350°F.

2. In small bowl with mixer at medium speed, beat cream cheese, ¼ cup sugar and 1 egg until smooth. Spread evenly in bottom of pie crust.

3. In same bowl beat ¼ cup sugar, remaining 2 eggs, the corn syrup, lemon juice, margarine, corn starch and grated lemon peel until well blended. Pour over cream cheese layer. Sprinkle remaining ¼ cup sugar evenly over filling.

4. Bake 50 to 55 minutes or until filling is puffed and set. Cool on wire rack. If desired, garnish with whipped cream, lemon peel and pastry cut-outs.

Makes 8 servings

Lemon-Raisin Chantilly Tart

1   **unbaked ready-made 9-inch pie crust**
2   **eggs**
3   **egg yolks**
6   **tablespoons sugar**
1   **teaspoon grated lemon peel**
½   **cup fresh lemon juice**
2   **tablespoons milk**
½   **teaspoon cornstarch**
6   **tablespoons unsalted butter or**
      margarine, cut into small chunks
1   **cup raisins**
1   **cup whipping cream, whipped and**
      lightly sweetened

Preheat oven to 400°F. Fit crust into 9-inch tart pan
with removable bottom, folding in excess dough to
reinforce side. Refrigerate 20 minutes. Prick dough all
over with fork. Line with foil and fill with uncooked
beans, rice or pie weights. Bake 12 minutes. Remove
foil and beans; continue to bake until tart shell is
golden brown and crisp, about 15 minutes. Cool
completely on wire rack.

Stir eggs, egg yolks, sugar, lemon peel and lemon juice
in heavy medium saucepan with wire whisk until well
blended. Combine milk and cornstarch in small cup;
stir into egg mixture. Add butter, whisking constantly
over medium-low heat until mixture coats back of
spoon, about 5 minutes. *Do not boil.* Stir in raisins;
remove from heat. Cool to room temperature. Spread
filling evenly in prepared tart shell. Pipe or dollop

whipped cream onto top of tart. Garnish with lemon peel, mint leaves and sugared raisins, if desired. Serve immediately or chill up to 2 hours before serving.

Makes 6 to 8 servings

Favorite recipe from **California Raisin Advisory Board**

Peanut Butter Cream Pie

¾ cup powdered sugar
⅓ cup creamy peanut butter
1 baked (9-inch) pie crust
1 cup milk
1 cup sour cream
1 package (4-serving size) instant French
    vanilla pudding and pie filling mix
5 peanut butter candy cups, divided
2 cups thawed nondairy whipped topping

1. Combine powdered sugar and peanut butter with fork in medium bowl until blended. Place evenly in bottom of pie crust.

2. Place milk and sour cream in large bowl. Add pudding mix. Beat with wire whisk or electric mixer 1 to 2 minutes until thickened.

3. Pour half of filling over peanut butter mixture. Coarsely chop 4 candy cups; sprinkle over filling. Top with remaining filling.

4. Spread whipped topping over filling. Cut remaining candy cup into 8 pieces; place on top of pie. Refrigerate.

Makes 8 servings

Fudgey Peanut Butter Chip Brownie Pie

2 eggs
1 teaspoon vanilla extract
1 cup sugar
½ cup (1 stick) butter or margarine, melted
½ cup all-purpose flour
⅓ cup HERSHEY¸S Cocoa
¼ teaspoon salt
⅔ cup REESE'S® Peanut Butter Chips
1 packaged butter-flavored crumb crust (6 ounces)
   Peanut Butter Sauce (recipe follows)
   Vanilla ice cream

Heat oven to 350°F. In small bowl, lightly beat eggs and vanilla; blend in sugar and butter. Stir together flour, cocoa and salt. Add to egg mixture; beat until blended. Stir in peanut butter chips. Place crust on baking sheet; pour chocolate mixture into crust. Bake 45 to 50 minutes or until set. Cool completely on wire rack. Prepare Peanut Butter Sauce; serve over pie and ice cream. *Makes 8 servings*

Peanut Butter Sauce

1 cup REESE'S® Peanut Butter Chips
⅓ cup milk
¼ cup whipping cream
¼ teaspoon vanilla extract

In small saucepan over low heat, combine peanut butter chips, milk and whipping cream. Cook, stirring constantly, until chips are melted and mixture is smooth. Remove from heat; stir in vanilla. Serve warm.

Chocolate Pie

½ cup reduced fat biscuit mix
3 tablespoons unsweetened cocoa powder, sifted
1¼ cups sugar
2 tablespoons margarine, melted
1 whole egg
3 egg whites
1½ teaspoons vanilla extract

1. Preheat oven to 350°F. Spray 9-inch pie pan with nonstick cooking spray. Set aside.

2. Combine biscuit mix, cocoa and sugar in large bowl; mix well. Add margarine, egg, egg whites and vanilla; mix well. Pour mixture into prepared pan.

3. Bake 40 minutes or until knife inserted in center comes out clean. Garnish with powdered sugar, if desired. *Makes 8 servings*

Fudgy Bittersweet Brownie Pie

12 squares (1 ounce each) bittersweet
   chocolate*
½ cup margarine or butter
2 eggs
½ cup sugar
1 cup all-purpose flour
½ teaspoon salt
1½ cups prepared hot fudge sauce, divided
1½ cups prepared caramel topping, divided
¾ cup chopped pecans, divided

1. Preheat oven to 350°F. Grease 10-inch tart pan with removable bottom or 9-inch square baking pan.

2. Melt chocolate and margarine in small heavy saucepan over low heat, stirring constantly; set aside.

3. Beat eggs in medium bowl with electric mixer at medium speed 30 seconds. Gradually beat in sugar; beat 1 minute. Beat in chocolate mixture, scraping down side of bowl once. Beat in flour and salt at low speed until just combined, scraping down side of bowl once. Spread mixture evenly in prepared pan.

4. Bake 25 minutes or until center is just set. Cool pie completely in pan on wire rack. To serve, cut pie into 12 wedges, or 12 squares if using square pan. Place fudge sauce in small microwavable bowl. Microwave at HIGH until hot, stirring once. Spoon 2 tablespoons *each* fudge sauce and caramel topping over each serving. Top with pecans.   *Makes 12 servings*

*Substitute 4 squares unsweetened chocolate *plus* 8 squares semisweet chocolate, if desired.

Mocha Ice Cream Pie

2 cups coffee or vanilla ice cream, softened

1 prepared (9-inch) chocolate crumb pie crust

1 jar (12 ounces) hot caramel ice cream topping, divided

2 cups chocolate ice cream, softened

2 cups thawed nondairy whipped topping

1 English toffee bar (1.4 ounces), chopped

1. Spread coffee ice cream in bottom of pie crust. Freeze 10 minutes or until semi-firm.

2. Spread half of caramel topping over coffee ice cream. Spread chocolate ice cream over caramel. Freeze 10 minutes or until semi-firm.

3. Spread remaining caramel topping over chocolate ice cream. Spoon whipped topping into pastry bag fitted with star decorating tip. Pipe rosettes on top of pie. Sprinkle toffee over topping.

4. Freeze pie until firm, 6 hours or overnight. Remove from freezer. Allow pie to stand at room temperature 15 minutes before serving.   *Makes 8 servings*

Variations: Experiment with different ice cream flavors and combinations, including rocky road, chocolate mint chip, pistachio and strawberry.

Brownie Pie à la Mode

½ cup sugar
2 tablespoons butter or margarine
2 tablespoons water
1⅓ cups HERSHEY₅S Semi-Sweet
 Chocolate Chips
2 eggs
⅔ cup all-purpose flour
¼ teaspoon baking soda
¼ teaspoon salt
1 teaspoon vanilla extract
¾ cup chopped nuts (optional)
 Fudge Sauce (recipe follows, optional)
 Ice cream, any flavor

Heat oven to 350°F. Grease 9-inch pie plate. In medium saucepan, combine sugar, butter and water. Cook over medium heat, stirring occasionally, just until mixture comes to a boil. Remove from heat. Immediately add chocolate chips; stir until melted. Add eggs; beat with spoon until well blended. Stir together flour, baking soda and salt. Add to chocolate mixture; stir until well blended. Stir in vanilla and nuts, if desired; pour into prepared pie plate. Bake 25 to 30 minutes or until almost set. (Pie will not test done in center.) Cool. Prepare Fudge Sauce, if desired. Top warm pie with scoops of ice cream and prepared sauce.

Makes 8 to 10 servings

Fudge Sauce

1 cup HERSHEY₂S Semi-Sweet
   Chocolate Chips
½ cup evaporated milk
¼ cup sugar
1 tablespoon butter or margarine

In medium microwave-safe bowl, combine all ingredients. Microwave at HIGH (100%) 1 minute; stir. If necessary, microwave at HIGH an additional 15 seconds at a time, stirring after each heating, just until chips are melted and mixture is smooth.

Chocolate Macaroon HEATH® Pie

½ cup butter or margarine, melted
3 cups shredded coconut
2 tablespoons all-purpose flour
1 package (6 ounces) HEATH® Bits
   or 1 heaping cupful crushed
   HEATH® Bar
½ gallon chocolate ice cream, softened

Preheat oven to 375°F. Combine butter, coconut and flour. Press into 9-inch pie pan. Bake at 375°F for 10 minutes or until edge is light golden brown. Cool to room temperature. Reserve ¼ cup HEATH® Bits and set aside. Combine ice cream and remaining HEATH® Bits. Spread over cooled crust. Sprinkle with reserved bits. Freeze at least 3 hours. Remove from freezer; let stand 10 minutes to soften before serving.

Makes 6 to 8 servings

Classic Pecan Pie

3 eggs
1 cup sugar
1 cup KARO® Light or Dark Corn Syrup
2 tablespoons MAZOLA® Margarine or
      butter, melted
1 teaspoon vanilla
1½ cups pecans
      Easy-As-Pie Crust (recipe follows) *or*
      1 (9-inch) frozen deep-dish pie
      crust*

1. Preheat oven to 350°F.

2. In medium bowl with fork beat eggs slightly. Add sugar, corn syrup, margarine and vanilla; stir until well blended. Stir in pecans. Pour into pie crust.

3. Bake 50 to 55 minutes or until knife inserted halfway between center and edge comes out clean. Cool on wire rack.   *Makes 8 servings*

*To use prepared frozen pie crust, do not thaw. Preheat oven and a cookie sheet. Pour filling into frozen crust. Bake on cookie sheet. (Insulated cookie sheet not recommended.)

Easy-As-Pie Crust

1¼ cups flour
⅛ teaspoon salt
½ cup MAZOLA® Margarine
2 tablespoons cold water

1. In bowl mix flour and salt. With pastry blender, cut in margarine until mixture resembles fine crumbs.

2. Sprinkle water over flour mixture while tossing with fork to blend well. Press dough firmly into ball.

3. On lightly floured surface roll out to 12-inch circle. Fit loosely into 9-inch pie plate. Trim and flute edge.

Makes one 9-inch pie crust

Praline Pie

1 (9-inch) HONEY MAID® Honey Graham
   Pie Crust
1 egg white, slightly beaten
¼ cup margarine, melted
1 cup firmly packed light brown sugar
¾ cup all-purpose flour
1 teaspoon DAVIS® Baking Powder
1 egg
1 teaspoon vanilla extract
1 cup PLANTERS® Pecans, chopped
   Prepared whipped topping, for garnish

Preheat oven to 375°F. Brush pie crust with egg white. Bake at 375°F for 5 minutes; set aside. *Decrease oven temperature to 350°F.*

In medium bowl, with electric mixer at low speed, beat margarine and brown sugar until blended. Mix in flour, baking powder, egg and vanilla until well combined. Stir in ¾ cup pecans. Spread into prepared crust; sprinkle top with remaining ¼ cup pecans. Bake at 350°F for 25 to 30 minutes or until lightly browned and filling is set. Cool completely on wire rack. Garnish with whipped topping.   *Makes 6 servings*

Turtle Nut Pie

3 eggs
1 cup KARO® Light Corn Syrup
⅔ cup sugar
⅓ cup (5⅓ tablespoons) MAZOLA®
    Margarine, melted
½ teaspoon salt
1 cup pecans
2 squares (1 ounce each) semisweet
    chocolate, melted ·
    Easy-As-Pie Crust (page 268) *or*
    1 (9-inch) frozen deep-dish pie
    crust*
½ cup caramel flavored topping for ice
    cream

1. Preheat oven to 350°F.

2. In medium bowl with fork, beat eggs slightly. Add corn syrup, sugar, margarine and salt; stir until well blended. Reserve ½ cup egg mixture; set aside.

3. Stir pecans and chocolate into remaining egg mixture; pour into pie crust.

4. Mix caramel topping and reserved egg mixture; carefully pour over pecan filling.

5. Bake 50 to 55 minutes or until filling is set about 3 inches from edge. Cool completely on wire rack.

Makes 8 servings

*To use prepared frozen pie crust, do not thaw. Preheat oven and a cookie sheet. Pour filling into frozen crust. Bake on cookie sheet. (Insulated cookie sheet not recommended.)

Black Bottom Banana Cream Pie

1 (9-inch) HONEY MAID® Honey Graham
  Pie Crust
1 egg white, slightly beaten
¼ cup heavy cream
4 (1-ounce) squares semisweet chocolate
¼ cup PLANTERS® Dry Roasted Peanuts,
  coarsely chopped
1 small banana, sliced
1 (4-serving size) package ROYAL®
  Instant Vanilla Pudding & Pie Filling
2 cups cold milk
  Whipped topping, for garnish
  Additional coarsely chopped
    PLANTERS® Dry Roasted Peanuts,
    for garnish

Preheat oven to 375°F. Brush pie crust with egg white.
Bake at 375°F for 5 minutes; set aside. In small
saucepan, over low heat, cook heavy cream and
chocolate until chocolate melts. Stir in peanuts.
Spread evenly into pie crust. Arrange banana slices
over chocolate; set aside. Prepare pudding according to
package directions for pie using cold milk; carefully
pour over bananas. Chill at least 2 hours. Garnish with
whipped topping and additional chopped peanuts.

Makes 8 servings

Raspberry Chocolate Mousse Pie

40 **chocolate wafer cookies**
½ **cup butter, melted**
7 **tablespoons sugar**
5 **egg yolks**
6 **squares (1 ounce each) semisweet chocolate, melted, cooled slightly**
3 **tablespoons raspberry-flavored liqueur (optional)**
3½ **cups thawed nondairy whipped topping Sweetened whipped cream, fresh raspberries and mint leaves (optional)**

1. Place cookies in food processor or blender; process with on/off pulses until finely crushed. Combine cookie crumbs and butter in medium bowl. Press onto bottom and 1 inch up side of 9-inch springform pan.

2. Combine ½ cup water and sugar in medium saucepan. Bring to a boil over medium-high heat. Boil 1 minute.

3. Place egg yolks in large bowl. Gradually whisk in hot sugar mixture. Return mixture to medium saucepan; whisk over low heat 1 to 2 minutes until mixture is thick and creamy. Remove from heat; pour mixture back into large bowl.

4. Whisk in melted chocolate and liqueur, if desired. Beat mixture until cool. Fold in whipped topping. Pour mixture into prepared crust. Freeze until firm. Allow pie to stand at room temperature 20 minutes before serving. Remove side of pan. Garnish with sweetened whipped cream, fresh raspberries and mint leaves, if desired. *Makes 10 servings*

OREO® Mud Pie

- 26 OREO® Chocolate Sandwich Cookies
- 2 tablespoons margarine, melted
- 1 pint chocolate ice cream, softened
- 2 pints coffee ice cream, softened
- ½ cup heavy cream, whipped
- ¼ cup PLANTERS® Walnuts, chopped
- ½ cup chocolate fudge topping

Finely crush 12 cookies; mix with margarine. Press crumb mixture onto bottom of 9-inch pie plate; stand remaining 14 cookies around edge of plate. Place in freezer for 10 minutes. Evenly spread chocolate ice cream into prepared crust. Scoop coffee ice cream into balls; arrange over chocolate layer. Freeze 4 hours or until firm. To serve, top with whipped cream, walnuts and fudge topping. *Makes 8 servings*

Mocha Cannoli Pie

2 cups (15 ounces) light ricotta cheese
½ cup sugar
1 tablespoon instant coffee powder
1 teaspoon vanilla extract
1 envelope unflavored gelatine
¼ cup water
½ cup mini semisweet chocolate chips
1 cup heavy cream, whipped
1 (9-inch) HONEY MAID® Honey Graham
      Pie Crust
   Additional whipped cream, chocolate-
      covered coffee beans and mint sprigs,
      for garnish

In large bowl, with mixer at medium speed, beat
ricotta, sugar, coffee powder and vanilla until light,
about 3 minutes. Meanwhile, in small saucepan,
sprinkle gelatine over water; let stand to soften
1 minute. Cook over medium-low heat, stirring
constantly, until gelatine completely dissolves. Stir
gelatine mixture and chocolate chips into ricotta
mixture; fold in whipped cream. Pour mixture into
crust. Refrigerate until set, about 3 hours. To serve,
garnish with whipped cream, coffee beans and mint
sprigs if desired.   *Makes 8 servings*

Chocolate-Almond Pudding Tarts

¾ cup sugar
⅓ cup HERSHEY₀S Cocoa
2 tablespoons cornstarch
2 tablespoons all-purpose flour
¼ teaspoon salt
1¾ cups milk
2 egg yolks, slightly beaten
2 tablespoons butter or margarine
¾ teaspoon vanilla extract
⅛ to ¼ teaspoon almond extract
6 single-serve graham cracker crumb
    crusts (4-ounce package)
    Whipped topping
    Sliced almonds

Microwave Directions: In medium microwave-safe bowl, stir together sugar, cocoa, cornstarch, flour and salt; gradually add milk and egg yolks, beating with whisk until smooth. Microwave at HIGH (100%) 5 minutes, stirring with whisk after each minute. Continue to microwave at HIGH 1 to 3 minutes or until mixture is smooth and very thick. Stir in butter, vanilla and almond extract. Spoon chocolate mixture equally into crusts. Press plastic wrap directly onto surface. Cool; refrigerate several hours. Just before serving, garnish with whipped topping and sliced almonds. Cover; refrigerate leftover tarts.

Makes 6 servings

Chocolate & Vanilla Swirl Tart

Tart Shell (recipe follows)
⅔ cup HERSHEY₅S Semi-Sweet
   Chocolate Chips
½ cup milk, divided
2 tablespoons sugar
½ teaspoon unflavored gelatin
1 tablespoon cold water
⅔ cup HERSHEY₅S Premier White Chips
1 teaspoon vanilla extract
1 cup (½ pint) cold whipping cream

Prepare Tart Shell. In small microwave-safe bowl, place chocolate chips, ¼ cup milk and sugar. Microwave at HIGH (100%) 1 minute; stir. If necessary, microwave at HIGH an additional 15 seconds at a time, stirring after each heating, just until chips are melted when stirred. Cool about 20 minutes. In small cup, sprinkle gelatin over water; let stand 2 minutes to soften. In second small microwave-safe bowl, place white chips and remaining ¼ cup milk. Microwave at HIGH 1 minute; stir. Add gelatin mixture and vanilla; stir until gelatin is dissolved. Cool about 20 minutes. In small bowl on high speed of electric mixer, beat whipping cream until stiff; fold 1 cup whipped cream into vanilla mixture. Fold remaining whipped cream into chocolate mixture. Alternately spoon chocolate and vanilla mixtures into prepared tart shell; swirl with knife for marbled effect. Refrigerate until firm. Cover; refrigerate leftover tart.

Makes 8 to 10 servings

Tart Shell

½ cup (1 stick) butter (do *not* use
     margarine), softened
2 tablespoons sugar
2 egg yolks
1 cup all-purpose flour

Heat oven to 375°F. Grease bottom and sides of fluted
8- or 9-inch tart pan. In small bowl, beat butter and
sugar until blended. Add egg yolks; mix well. Stir in
flour until mixture is crumbly. Press onto bottom and
up sides of prepared pan. (If dough is sticky, sprinkle
with 1 tablespoon flour.) Prick bottom with fork to
prevent puffing. Bake 8 to 10 minutes or until lightly
browned. Cool completely.

Extra-Special

GRAND FINALES

Chocolate Fluted Kiss Cups

1½ cups HERSHEY₂S MINI CHIPS₈ Semi-
     Sweet Chocolate *or* 1 HERSHEY₂S
     Milk Chocolate Bar (7 ounces),
     broken into pieces
     Peanut Butter Filling (recipe follows)
24   HERSHEY₈S KISSES₈ Milk Chocolates

Microwave Directions: Line small muffin cups (1¾ inches in diameter) with small paper bake cups. In small microwave-safe bowl, place small chocolate chips. Microwave at HIGH (100%) 1 minute; stir. If necessary, microwave at HIGH an additional 15 seconds at a time, stirring after each heating, just until chips are melted when stirred. With small brush, coat inside of paper cups with melted chocolate. Refrigerate 20 minutes; coat any thin spots. Refrigerate until firm, preferably overnight. Gently peel paper from chocolate cups. Prepare Peanut Butter Filling; spoon into cups. Cover; refrigerate before serving. Remove wrappers from chocolate pieces. Before serving, top each cup with chocolate piece.   *Makes about 24 servings*

Peanut Butter Filling

1 cup REESE'S₈ Creamy Peanut Butter
1 cup powdered sugar
1 tablespoon butter or margarine,
   softened

In small bowl, beat peanut butter, powdered sugar and butter until smooth.

After-Dinner Mocha Truffle Cups

36 Chocolate Cups (recipe follows) or
     purchased chocolate liqueur cups
1 cup whipping cream
2 eggs
1 package (6 ounces) semisweet
     chocolate chips (1 cup)
2 tablespoons prepared espresso, cooled
1 tablespoon coffee-flavored liqueur
1 teaspoon unflavored gelatin
     Sweetened whipped cream
     Chocolate-covered coffee beans and
      fresh mint leaves (optional)

1. Prepare Chocolate Cups; set aside.

2. Pour cream into large chilled bowl. Beat with electric mixer at high speed until soft peaks form; refrigerate.

3. Place eggs in separate large bowl; beat with electric mixer at high speed about 5 minutes or until thick and lemon colored. Melt chocolate chips in double boiler; stir until chips are melted. Remove from heat. Add ¼ cup melted chocolate to beaten eggs; stir to blend. Stir egg mixture into remaining melted chocolate. Cook over medium heat 1 minute, stirring constantly. Remove from heat.

4. Place espresso and liqueur in small saucepan; sprinkle with gelatin. Let stand 1 minute to soften. Heat over low heat until gelatin is completely dissolved, stirring constantly.

5. Gradually add gelatin mixture, a few drops at a time, to chocolate mixture, whisking until smooth.

6. Gently fold ½ of chocolate mixture into chilled whipped cream. Add to remaining chocolate, gently folding until combined.

7. Spoon chocolate mixture into reserved Chocolate Cups, filling to top; refrigerate at least 3 hours or until firm. To serve, dollop with whipped cream. Garnish with coffee beans and mint leaves, if desired.

Makes 36 candy cups (about 1½ pounds)

Chocolate Cups

1 **package (12 ounces) semi-sweet chocolate chips (2 cups)**
1 **tablespoon vegetable shortening**

1. Melt chips with shortening in heavy small saucepan over low heat, stirring *constantly* to prevent scorching. Remove from heat. Spoon about ½ tablespoon melted chocolate into each of 36 small foil candy cups. Brush chocolate up side of each cup with clean paintbrush, coating foil completely.

2. Carefully wipe off any chocolate that may have run over top of foil cup using tip of finger. Place cups on baking sheet; let stand in cool place until firm. (Do not refrigerate.)

3. Cut slits in bottom of foil cups and peel foil up from bottom. *Makes 36 cups*

Berry Delicious Trifles

1 package (4-serving size) instant vanilla
    pudding and pie filling mix
2¼ cups milk
1 cup sliced strawberries
1 cup raspberries
1 cup blueberries
1 frozen pound cake (10¾ ounces),
    thawed
2 tablespoons orange-flavored liqueur or
    orange juice
¼ cup orange marmalade
    Sweetened whipped cream and mint
    leaves (optional)

1. Beat pudding mix and milk in medium bowl with
electric mixer at low speed 2 minutes; set aside.
Combine strawberries, raspberries and blueberries in
medium bowl; set aside.

2. Slice cake into 12 slices, each about ½ inch wide.
Brush one side of each piece with liqueur; spread
marmalade over liqueur.

3. Cut cake slices in half lengthwise. Place 4 pieces of
cake each against side of 6 martini or parfait glasses
with marmalade side toward center of glass.

4. Place ¼ cup berries in bottom of each glass; top each
with heaping ⅓ cup pudding mixture and then ¼ cup
berries. Refrigerate 30 minutes. Garnish with
sweetened whipped cream and mint leaves, if desired.

Makes 6 servings

Fresh Fruit Trifle

------

    2   **cups skim milk**
    2   **tablespoons cornstarch**
    ⅓   **cup sugar**
    4   **egg whites, lightly beaten**
    2   **teaspoons vegetable oil**
   1½   **teaspoons vanilla extract**
    6   **tablespoons sherry or apple juice,
          divided**
    4   **cups cubed angel food cake**
    6   **cups diced assorted fruits (apricots,
          peaches, nectarines, plums and
          berries)**

1. For custard, combine milk and cornstarch in medium saucepan; stir until cornstarch is dissolved. Add sugar, egg whites and oil; mix well. Bring to a boil over medium-low heat, stirring constantly with wire whisk; boil until thickened. Remove from heat. Cool. Stir in vanilla and 2 tablespoons sherry.

2. Place one-third cake pieces in bottom of 2-quart glass bowl or trifle dish. Sprinkle with one-third remaining sherry. Spoon ⅔ cup custard over cake. Spoon one-third fruit over custard. Repeat process twice, ending with fruit. Serve immediately.

Makes 12 servings

Traditional Tiramisu

1 recipe Zabaglione (recipe follows)
⅔ cup whipping cream, chilled
4 tablespoons sugar, divided
1 pound mascarpone cheese* (about
   2¼ cups)
⅓ cup freshly brewed espresso or strong
   coffee
¼ cup Cognac or brandy
1 tablespoon vanilla extract
3 packages (3 ounces each) ladyfingers,
   split
3 ounces bittersweet or semisweet
   chocolate, grated
1 tablespoon cocoa powder

*Mascarpone is available at Italian markets and some specialty
stores. If unavailable, blend 2 (8-ounce) packages softened cream
cheese with ½ cup whipping cream and 5 tablespoons sour cream.

1. Prepare Zabaglione. Cover; refrigerate until chilled.

2. Beat cream with 2 tablespoons sugar in large bowl
until soft peaks form. Gently fold in mascarpone
cheese, then Zabaglione. (Make sure Zabaglione is well
mixed before adding.) Refrigerate 3 hours.

3. Combine espresso, Cognac, remaining 2 tablespoons
sugar and vanilla extract.

4. Layer ¼ of ladyfingers in flower-petal design in
2-quart glass bowl with straight sides or trifle dish.
Generously brush ladyfingers with espresso mixture.
Spoon ¼ of cheese mixture over ladyfingers to within
1 inch of side of bowl. Sprinkle with ¼ of chocolate.

5. Repeat layers 3 more times using remaining ladyfingers, espresso mixture, cheese mixture and grated chocolate. (For garnish, sprinkle remaining ¼ of grated chocolate around edge of dessert, if desired.) Sift cocoa powder over top with small sieve. Cover; refrigerate until chilled.   *Makes 8 to 10 servings*

Zabaglione

5 **egg yolks**
¼ **cup sugar**
½ **cup marsala wine, divided**
¼ **cup dry white wine**

1. Place egg yolks in top of double boiler; add sugar. Beat until mixture is pale yellow and creamy.

2. Place water in bottom of double boiler. Bring to a boil over high heat; reduce heat to low. Place top of double boiler over simmering water. Gradually beat ¼ cup marsala into egg yolk mixture. Beat 1 minute. Gradually beat in remaining ¼ cup marsala and white wine.

3. Continue cooking custard over gently simmering water 6 to 10 minutes until mixture is fluffy and thick enough to form soft mounds when dropped from beaters, beating constantly and scraping bottom and sides of pan frequently. (Watch carefully and *do not overcook* or custard will curdle.) Immediately remove top of double boiler from water. Whisk custard briefly.**   *Makes 4 servings*

**Zabaglione can be served as its own recipe. Pour into 4 individual serving dishes. Serve immediately with fresh berries and/or cookies.

Easy Tiramisu

2 **packages (3 ounces each) ladyfingers, thawed if frozen, split in half horizontally**
¾ **cup brewed espresso***
2 **tablespoons coffee liqueur or brandy (optional)**
1 **package (8 ounces) cream cheese, softened**
2 **tablespoons sugar**
⅓ **cup sour cream**
½ **cup whipping cream**
2 **tablespoons unsweetened cocoa powder, divided**
Chocolate curls and mint leaves (optional)

*Use fresh brewed espresso, instant espresso powder prepared according to directions on jar or 2 teaspoons instant coffee powder dissolved in ¾ cup hot water.

1. Place ladyfingers on baking sheet, uncovered, 8 hours or overnight to dry. Or, dry ladyfingers by placing on microwavable plate. Microwave at MEDIUM-HIGH (70% power) 1 minute, turn ladyfingers over. Microwave at MEDIUM-HIGH 1 to 1½ minutes until dry.

2. Combine espresso and liqueur, if desired, in small bowl. Dip half the ladyfingers in espresso mixture; place in bottom of 2-quart serving bowl.

3. Beat cream cheese and sugar with electric mixer at medium speed until fluffy; add sour cream, beating until blended. Add whipping cream, beating until smooth. Spread half the cheese mixture over ladyfingers.

4. Place 1 tablespoon cocoa in fine strainer. Lightly tap rim of strainer and dust cocoa over cheese layer.

5. Dip remaining ladyfingers in espresso mixture. Place over cheese mixture in serving bowl.

6. Spread remaining cheese mixture over ladyfingers. Dust remaining 1 tablespoon cocoa over cheese layer. Refrigerate, covered, 4 hours or overnight. Garnish with chocolate curls and mint leaves, if desired.

Makes 6 servings

Tiramisu

- 6 egg yolks
- ½ cup sugar
- ⅓ cup Cognac or brandy
- 2 cups (15 ounces) SARGENTO® Old Fashioned Ricotta Cheese
- 1 cup whipping cream, whipped
- 32 ladyfingers, split in half
- 3 teaspoons instant coffee dissolved in ¾ cup boiling water
- 1 tablespoon unsweetened cocoa Chocolate curls (optional)

In top of double boiler, whisk together egg yolks, sugar and Cognac. Place pan over simmering water in bottom of double boiler. Cook, whisking constantly, about 2 to 3 minutes until mixture is thickened. Remove top of double boiler; cool yolk mixture completely. In large bowl of electric mixer, beat yolk mixture and Ricotta cheese on medium speed until blended. Fold in whipped cream.

Place half the ladyfingers in bottom of 13×9-inch pan, cut sides up. Brush with half the coffee; spread with half the Ricotta mixture. Repeat layers. Refrigerate 2 hours. Just before serving, dust with cocoa using fine sieve; cut into squares. Garnish with chocolate curls, if desired. *Makes 16 servings*

Banana Chocolate Chip Parfaits

1 package DUNCAN HINES® Chocolate
    Chip Cookie Mix

PUDDING

3 tablespoons cornstarch
¼ teaspoon salt
1⅔ cups water
1 can (14 ounces) sweetened condensed
    milk
3 egg yolks, beaten
2 tablespoons butter or margarine
1½ teaspoons vanilla extract
3 ripe bananas, sliced
    Whipped topping, for garnish

1. Preheat oven to 375°F. Grease 13×9×2-inch pan.
Prepare cookie mix following package directions.
Spread in pan. Bake at 375°F for 15 to 18 minutes or
until edges are light golden brown. Cool.

2. For pudding, combine cornstarch, salt and water in
medium saucepan. Add sweetened condensed milk and
egg yolks. Cook over medium heat, stirring constantly,
until thickened. Remove from heat. Stir in butter and
vanilla extract. Cool.

3. To assemble, cut outer edges from cookie bars.
Crumble to make 1¾ cups crumbs. Cut remaining
cookie bars into 1×2-inch pieces. Layer pudding,
banana slices and crumbs in parfait dishes. Repeat
layers 1 or 2 more times ending with pudding. Garnish
with whipped topping. Refrigerate until ready to serve.
Serve with bars. *Makes 6 parfaits*

Original Banana Pudding

½ cup sugar
3 tablespoons all-purpose flour
   Dash salt
4 eggs
2 cups milk
½ teaspoon vanilla extract
43 NILLA® Wafers
5 to 6 ripe bananas, sliced (about 4 cups)

Reserve 2 tablespoons sugar. In top of double boiler, combine remaining sugar, flour and salt. Beat in 1 whole egg and 3 egg yolks; reserve 3 egg whites. Stir in milk. Cook, uncovered, over boiling water, stirring constantly 10 minutes or until thickened. Remove from heat; stir in vanilla.

In bottom of 1½-quart round casserole, spoon ½ cup custard; cover with 8 wafers. Top with generous layer of sliced bananas; pour ⅔ cup custard over bananas. Arrange 10 wafers around outside edge of dish; cover custard with 11 wafers. Top with sliced bananas and ⅔ cup custard. Cover custard with 14 wafers; top with sliced bananas and remaining custard.

In small bowl, with electric mixer at high speed, beat reserved egg whites until soft peaks form. Gradually add reserved 2 tablespoons sugar, beating until mixture forms stiff peaks. Spoon on top of custard, spreading to cover entire surface.

Bake at 425°F for 5 minutes, or until surface is lightly browned. Garnish with additional banana slices if desired. Serve warm or cold.   *Makes 8 servings*

Rice Pudding Tarts

1 **cup cooked rice**
1 **cup low-fat milk**
⅓ **cup sugar**
¼ **cup raisins**
⅛ **teaspoon salt**
2 **eggs, beaten**
¾ **cup heavy cream**
½ **teaspoon vanilla extract**
¼ **teaspoon almond extract**
6 **frozen tartlet pastry shells, partially**
  baked and cooled
⅛ **teaspoon ground nutmeg for garnish**
  Fresh berries for garnish
  Fresh mint for garnish

Combine rice, milk, sugar, raisins and salt in medium
saucepan. Cook over medium-low heat 30 to 35
minutes or until thick and creamy, stirring frequently.
Remove from heat; add one-fourth rice mixture to
eggs. Return egg mixture to saucepan; stir in cream
and extracts. Spoon equally into pastry shells; sprinkle
with nutmeg. Place tarts on baking sheet. Bake at
350°F 20 to 30 minutes or until pudding is set. Cool on
wire rack 1 hour. Use knife to loosen pastries from
aluminum containers; unmold. Garnish with berries
and mint. Serve at room temperature. Refrigerate
remaining tarts.   *Makes 6 servings*

Favorite recipe from **USA Rice Council**

Apple Raisin Risotto

3 tablespoons margarine, divided
1 large Golden Delicious apple, peeled, cored and diced
¾ cup arborio rice
⅓ cup raisins
¼ cup frozen unsweetened apple juice concentrate, thawed
1 cup unsweetened apple juice, divided
1 tablespoon packed dark brown sugar
½ teaspoon ground cinnamon
1 can (12 ounces) evaporated skimmed milk
1½ cups skim milk
1½ teaspoons vanilla extract

1. Melt 2 tablespoons margarine in large, heavy saucepan over medium heat. Add apple. Cook and stir until apple is fork-tender. Add rice; stir until grains become shiny. Add raisins and apple juice concentrate. Cook and stir until all of concentrate is absorbed.

2. Add ½ cup apple juice. Cook and stir until most of juice is absorbed. Add remaining ½ cup apple juice. Cook and stir until most of juice is absorbed. Add sugar and cinnamon; mix well. Reduce heat to low.

3. Combine evaporated milk and skim milk in medium saucepan. Heat over medium heat just until mixture becomes warm. *Do not boil.* Remove from heat.

4. Add ½ cup milk mixture to rice mixture. Cook and stir until most of milk is absorbed; repeat until all milk mixture is used. Do not allow last addition of milk to be completely absorbed. Remove from heat. Stir in remaining 1 tablespoon margarine and vanilla. Serve immediately. *Makes 8 servings*

Mocha Meringue Pudding

- 3 **cups cooked rice**
- 3½ **cups low-fat milk, divided**
- ⅔ **cup sugar, divided**
- ½ **teaspoon salt**
- 3 **eggs, separated**
- 1½ **teaspoons vanilla extract, divided**
- 4 **bars (1.55 ounces each) milk chocolate, broken in squares**
- 1 **tablespoon instant coffee**

Combine rice, 3 cups milk, ⅓ cup sugar and salt in large saucepan. Cook over medium heat 20 to 25 minutes or until thick and creamy, stirring frequently. Beat egg yolks and remaining ½ cup milk in small bowl. Stir into rice mixture and cook 3 minutes more. Remove from heat. Stir in 1 teaspoon vanilla. Spread into buttered 9×9-inch baking pan. Arrange chocolate bars over rice mixture. Beat egg whites in medium bowl with electric mixer until soft peaks form. Add remaining ⅓ cup sugar, 1 tablespoon at a time, about 4 minutes or until stiff glossy peaks form. Fold in coffee and remaining ½ teaspoon vanilla. Spread over pudding. Bake at 350°F 15 minutes or until golden brown. Serve warm. *Makes 6 servings*

Favorite recipe from **USA Rice Council**

Honey Bread Pudding

8 cups day-old egg bread cubes
3 cups milk
1 cup half-and-half
6 eggs, beaten
½ cup honey
1 tablespoon grated orange peel
1 teaspoon vanilla
1 teaspoon ground cinnamon
  Honey Cream Sauce (recipe follows)

Arrange bread in bottom of lightly greased shallow 2-quart baking dish. Stir together milk and half-and-half in large bowl; beat in eggs, honey, orange peel, vanilla and cinnamon, mixing well. Pour mixture over bread cubes in baking dish and let stand 1 hour or until liquid is absorbed by bread.

Bake in preheated 375°F oven 45 to 50 minutes or until knife inserted near center comes out clean. Serve with Honey Cream Sauce.

Makes 8 to 12 servings

Note: Recipe can be halved; use lightly greased 1-quart baking dish and bake pudding 40 to 45 minutes or until knife inserted near center comes out clean.

Honey Cream Sauce

1 cup whipping cream
¼ cup honey
1 tablespoon rum *or* ½ teaspoon rum flavoring

Beat cream in medium bowl with electric mixer until soft peaks form; slowly beat in honey and beat until mixture forms stiff peaks. Fold in rum.

Makes about 2 cups

Favorite recipe from **National Honey Board**

Old-Fashioned Bread Pudding

- 2 **cups skim milk**
- 4 **egg whites**
- 3 **tablespoons sugar**
- 2 **tablespoons margarine, melted**
- 1 **tablespoon vanilla extract**
- 2 **teaspoons ground cinnamon**
- 12 **slices whole wheat bread, cut into ½-inch cubes**
- ½ **cup raisins**
- ½ **cup chopped dried apples**

1. Preheat oven to 350°F. Spray 2-quart casserole with nonstick cooking spray. Set aside. Combine milk, egg whites, sugar, margarine, vanilla and cinnamon in large bowl; mix well. Add bread, raisins and dried apples. Allow to stand 5 minutes.

2. Pour mixture into prepared casserole dish. Bake 35 minutes or until well browned. Cool in pan on wire rack.

Makes 12 servings

Tropical Bread Pudding with Orange Sauce

¾ **cup raisins**
3 **cups milk**
3 **eggs**
1 **cup sugar**
1 **cup shredded coconut**
⅔ **cup coarsely chopped walnuts**
3 **tablespoons butter, melted**
2 **tablespoons vanilla extract**
1 **teaspoon ground nutmeg**
1 **jar (8 ounces) maraschino cherries,**
    undrained
1 **can (11 ounces) mandarin orange**
    segments, undrained
1 **loaf (16 ounces) cinnamon-raisin bread**
    Orange Sauce (recipe follows)

1. Preheat oven to 350°F. Lightly spray 13×9-inch baking pan with cooking spray.

2. Place raisins in small bowl. Pour boiling water over to cover. Let stand 2 to 3 minutes until plump. Drain.

3. Combine raisins, milk, eggs, sugar, coconut, walnuts, butter, vanilla and nutmeg in large bowl; mix well. Add cherries and oranges with liquid; mix well.

4. Break bread into large pieces, about 2 inches square. Add bread pieces to milk mixture. Mixture should be moist but not soupy. Pour into prepared pan. Sprinkle with additional coconut, if desired.

5. Bake 1 hour to 1 hour and 15 minutes or until knife inserted near center comes out clean. Serve with Orange Sauce.   *Makes 10 to 12 servings*

Orange Sauce

1½ **cups powdered sugar**
½ **cup butter, melted**
¼ **cup whipping cream**
1 **egg yolk**
2 **tablespoons orange-flavored liqueur**

1. Combine powdered sugar, butter and cream in medium saucepan. Add egg yolk; mix well with wire whisk. Cook over medium heat, stirring constantly, until thickened.

2. Remove from heat and add liqueur. Let cool slightly.

Blueberry Bread Pudding with Caramel Sauce

8   slices white bread, cubed
1   cup fresh or frozen blueberries
2   cups skim milk
1   cup EGG BEATERS® Healthy Real Egg
      Product
⅔   cup sugar
1   teaspoon vanilla extract
¼   teaspoon ground cinnamon
      Caramel Sauce (recipe follows)

Place bread cubes in bottom of lightly greased
8×8×2-inch baking pan. Sprinkle with blueberries; set
aside.

In large bowl, combine milk, EGG BEATERS®, sugar,
vanilla and cinnamon; pour over bread mixture. Set
pan in larger pan filled with 1-inch depth hot water.
Bake at 350°F for 1 hour or until knife inserted in
center comes out clean. Serve warm with Caramel
Sauce.   *Makes 9 servings*

Caramel Sauce: In small saucepan, over low heat,
heat ¼ cup skim milk and 14 vanilla caramels until
caramels are melted, stirring frequently.

Crème Caramel

- ½ **cup sugar, divided**
- 1 **tablespoon hot water**
- 2 **cups skim milk**
- ⅛ **teaspoon salt**
- ½ **cup cholesterol-free egg substitute**
- ½ **teaspoon vanilla extract**
- ⅛ **teaspoon maple extract**

1. Heat ¼ cup sugar in heavy saucepan over low heat, stirring constantly until melted and caramel colored. Remove from heat; stir in hot water. Return to heat; stir 5 minutes until mixture is a dark caramel color. Divide melted sugar evenly among 6 custard cups. Set aside.

2. Preheat oven to 350°F. Combine milk, remaining ¼ cup sugar and salt in medium bowl. Add egg substitute and extracts; mix well. Pour ½ cup mixture into each custard cup. Place cups in heavy pan; pour hot water into pan to 1- to 2-inch depth. Bake 40 to 45 minutes until knife inserted near edge of cup comes out clean. Cool on wire rack. Refrigerate at least 4 hours or overnight.

3. When ready to serve, run knife around edge of custard cup. Invert custard onto serving plate; remove cup. *Makes 6 servings*

Raspberry Flan

1½ cups milk
  3 eggs, slightly beaten
  ¼ cup honey
  1 teaspoon grated orange peel
     Raspberry Sauce (recipe follows)
     Raspberries and mint sprigs for garnish
        (optional)

Combine milk, eggs, honey and orange peel in medium
bowl; stir until blended. Pour into four ½-cup buttered
molds or one 3-cup mold. Place molds on rack in pan
of hot water.

Bake in preheated 300°F oven 15 to 20 minutes for
½-cup molds or 30 to 40 minutes for 3-cup mold or
until custard is set and knife blade inserted near center
comes out clean.

Cool at room temperature, then refrigerate 2 hours.
Run thin blade around edge to loosen; invert flan onto
serving plate. Spoon Raspberry Sauce over each
serving. Garnish with raspberries and mint sprig, if
desired.   *Makes 4 servings*

Raspberry Sauce

  2 cups fresh or thawed frozen
        raspberries*
  2 tablespoons honey
  ½ teaspoon grated orange peel

*Substitute blackberries, strawberries or blueberries for raspberries,
if desired.

Reserve 12 whole berries and set aside for garnish, if desired. Place remainder in blender or food processor; process until puréed. Sieve to remove seeds, if desired. Combine purée with honey and orange peel in small bowl.   *Makes about ¾ cup*

Favorite recipe from **National Honey Board**

Cherry Turnovers

- 8 **frozen phyllo dough sheets, thawed**
- ¼ **cup butter or margarine, melted**
- 6 **tablespoons no-sugar-added black cherry fruit spread**
- 1½ **tablespoons cherry-flavored liqueur (optional)**
- 1 **egg**
- 1 **teaspoon cold water**

1. Preheat oven to 400°F. Lightly brush each phyllo sheet with butter; stack. Cut through all sheets to form six (5-inch) squares.

2. Combine fruit spread and cherry liqueur, if desired. Place 1 tablespoon fruit spread mixture in center of each stack of eight phyllo squares; brush edges of phyllo with butter. Fold edges over to form triangle; gently press edges together to seal. Place on ungreased cookie sheet.

3. Beat together egg and water; brush over phyllo triangles. Bake 10 minutes or until golden brown. Cool on wire rack. Serve warm or at room temperature.

Makes 6 turnovers

Raspberry Napoleon

Butter-flavored nonstick cooking spray
4 sheets phyllo dough, divided
Napoleon Filling (recipe follows)
2 cups fresh or frozen raspberries,
thawed, drained, divided

1. Preheat oven to 375°F. Spray cookie sheet with butter-flavored nonstick cooking spray.

2. Place 1 sheet of phyllo on waxed paper. Cover remaining sheets with damp kitchen towel to prevent dough from drying out. Set aside. Spray phyllo with butter-flavored cooking spray. Cut phyllo into thirds lengthwise. Carefully fold 1 third in half; spray with cooking spray. Fold in half again; spray. Fold in half again forming rectangle; spray top with cooking spray. Place on prepared cookie sheet. Repeat folding and spraying with remaining 2 thirds.

3. Repeat step 2 with remaining phyllo dough.

4. Bake 7 to 9 minutes until phyllo is golden brown. Cool on wire rack. Prepare Napoleon Filling.

5. Spread 2 tablespoons Napoleon Filling on each of 4 phyllo rectangles. Place, filling sides up, on dessert plates. Top each with ¼ cup raspberries.

6. Spread 2 tablespoons Napoleon Filling on each of 4 more phyllo rectangles. Place, filling sides down, on top of raspberry layer. Spread top of each stack with 2 tablespoons Napoleon Filling. Top each with ¼ cup raspberries, reserving 4 raspberries for garnish.

7. Spread each of remaining 4 rectangles with 2 tablespoons Napoleon Filling. Place, filling sides down, on raspberry layer. Top each stack with 1 tablespoon Napoleon Filling and 1 raspberry.

Makes 4 servings

Napoleon Filling

1 **container (15 ounces) low-fat ricotta cheese**
1 **container (15 ounces) nonfat ricotta cheese**
3 **tablespoons sugar**
1 **teaspoon vanilla extract**
½ **teaspoon lemon extract**

Place both cheeses, sugar and extracts in food processor or blender; process until smooth.

Raspberry Cheesecake Blossoms

3 packages (10 ounces each) frozen
raspberries, thawed
¼ cup butter, melted
8 sheets phyllo dough*
1 package (8 ounces) cream cheese,
softened
½ cup cottage cheese
1 egg
½ cup plus 3 tablespoons sugar, divided
4 teaspoons lemon juice, divided
½ teaspoon vanilla extract
Fresh raspberries and sliced kiwifruit
(optional)

1. Drain thawed raspberries in fine-meshed sieve over 1-cup glass measure. Reserve liquid.

2. Preheat oven to 350°F. Grease 12 (2½-inch) muffin cups.

3. Brush melted butter onto 1 phyllo sheet. Cover with second phyllo sheet; brush with butter. Repeat with remaining sheets of phyllo.

4. Cut stack of phyllo dough in thirds lengthwise and then in fourths crosswise, to make a total of 12 squares. Gently fit each stacked square into one prepared muffin cup.

5. Place cream cheese, cottage cheese, egg, 3 tablespoons sugar, 1 teaspoon lemon juice and vanilla in food processor or blender container. Process until smooth. Divide mixture evenly among blossom cups.

6. Bake 10 to 15 minutes until lightly browned. Carefully remove from muffin cups to wire racks to cool.

7. Bring reserved raspberry syrup to a boil in small saucepan over medium-high heat. Cook until reduced to ¾ cup, stirring occasionally.

8. Place thawed raspberries in food processor or blender container. Process until smooth. Press through fine-meshed sieve with back of spoon to remove seeds.

9. Combine raspberry purée, reduced syrup, remaining ½ cup sugar and 3 teaspoons lemon juice in small bowl. Mix well.

10. To serve, spoon raspberry sauce onto 12 dessert plates. Place cheesecake blossom on each plate. Garnish with raspberries and kiwi, if desired.

Makes 12 servings

*Cover with damp kitchen towel to prevent dough from drying out.

Honey Sopaipillas

¼ **cup plus 2 teaspoons sugar, divided**
½ **teaspoon ground cinnamon**
2 **cups all-purpose flour**
2 **teaspoons baking powder**
½ **teaspoon salt**
2 **tablespoons shortening**
¾ **cup warm water**
   Vegetable oil for deep-frying
   Honey

1. Combine ¼ cup sugar and cinnamon in small bowl; reserve. Combine flour, remaining 2 teaspoons sugar, baking powder and salt in medium bowl. With pastry blender or 2 knives, cut in shortening until mixture resembles fine crumbs. Gradually add water; stir with fork until mixture forms dough. Turn out onto lightly floured board; knead 2 minutes or until smooth. Shape into ball; cover with bowl and let rest 30 minutes.

2. Divide dough into 4 equal portions; shape each into ball. Flatten each ball into circle, 8 inches in diameter and ⅛ inch thick. Cut each round into 4 wedges.

3. Pour oil into electric skillet, deep heavy saucepan or Dutch oven to depth of 1½ inches. Heat oil to 360°F on deep-fry thermometer. Cook dough, two pieces at a time, 2 minutes or until puffed and golden brown, turning once during cooking. Remove from oil with slotted spoon; drain on paper towels. Sprinkle with reserved cinnamon-sugar mixture while still hot. Repeat with remaining sopaipillas. Serve hot with honey. *Makes 16 sopaipillas*

Apple Strudel

1   sheet (½ of a 17¼-ounce package) frozen puff pastry
1   cup (4 ounces) shredded ALPINE LACE® Reduced Sodium Muenster Cheese
2   large Granny Smith apples, peeled, cored and sliced ⅛ inch thick (12 ounces)
⅓   cup golden raisins
2   tablespoons apple brandy (optional)
¼   cup granulated sugar
¼   cup packed light brown sugar
½   teaspoon ground cinnamon
2   tablespoons unsalted butter substitute, melted

1. To shape the pastry: Thaw the pastry for 20 minutes. Preheat the oven to 350°F. On a floured board, roll out the pastry into a 15×12-inch rectangle.

2. To make the filling: Sprinkle the cheese over the pastry, leaving a 1-inch border. Arrange the apples on top. Sprinkle with the raisins, then the brandy, if you wish. In a small cup, mix both of the sugars with the cinnamon, then sprinkle over the apple filling.

3. Starting from one of the wide ends, roll up jelly-roll style. Place on a baking sheet, seam side down, tucking the ends under. Using a sharp knife, make 7 diagonal slits on the top, then brush with the butter. Bake for 35 minutes or until golden brown.

Makes 18 servings

Cannoli Pastries

18 to 20 Cannoli Pastry Shells (recipe
      follows)
 2 pounds ricotta cheese
1½ cups sifted powdered sugar
 2 teaspoons ground cinnamon
 ¼ cup diced candied orange peel, minced
 1 teaspoon grated lemon peel
      Powdered sugar
 2 ounces semisweet chocolate, finely
      chopped

1. Prepare Cannoli Pastry Shells; set aside.

2. For cannoli filling, beat cheese in large bowl with
electric mixer at medium speed until smooth. Add 1½
cups powdered sugar and cinnamon; beat at high speed
3 minutes. Add candied orange peel and lemon peel to
cheese mixture; mix well. Cover and refrigerate until
ready to serve.

3. To assemble, spoon cheese filling into pastry bag
fitted with large plain tip. Pipe about ¼ cup filling into
each reserved Cannoli Pastry Shell.* Roll Cannoli
Pastries in additional powdered sugar to coat. Dip ends
of pastries into chocolate. Arrange pastries on serving
plate. Garnish as desired.

Makes 18 to 20 pastries

*Do not fill Cannoli Pastry Shells ahead of time or shells will become
soggy.

Cannoli Pastry Shells

1¾ cups all-purpose flour
 2 tablespoons granulated sugar
 1 teaspoon grated lemon peel
 2 tablespoons butter or margarine
 1 egg
 6 tablespoons marsala wine
   Vegetable oil

1. Mix flour, granulated sugar and lemon peel in medium bowl; cut in butter with pastry blender or 2 knives until mixture resembles fine crumbs. Beat egg and marsala in small bowl; add to flour mixture. Stir with fork to form ball. Divide dough in half; shape into two 1-inch-thick square pieces. Wrap in plastic wrap and refrigerate at least 1 hour.

2. Heat 1½ inches oil in large saucepan to 325°F. Working with 1 piece of dough at a time, roll out on lightly floured surface to ⅟₁₆-inch thickness. Cut dough with knife into 9 or 10 (4×3-inch) rectangles. Wrap each rectangle around a greased metal cannoli form or an uncooked cannelloni pasta shell. Brush one edge of rectangle lightly with water; overlap with other edge and press firmly to seal.

3. Fry 2 or 3 cannoli pastry shells at a time, 1 to 1½ minutes until light brown, turning once. Remove; drain on paper towels. Cool until easy to handle. Carefully remove fried pastries from cannoli forms or pasta shells; cool completely. Repeat with remaining piece of dough.

Rich Chocolate Glazed Cream Puffs

1 cup water
½ cup (1 stick) butter or margarine
¼ teaspoon salt
1 cup all-purpose flour
4 eggs
Chocolate Cream Filling (recipe follows)
Rich Chocolate Glaze (recipe follows)
Fresh strawberries (optional)

Heat oven to 400°F. Lightly grease cookie sheet. In medium saucepan, heat water, butter and salt to full rolling boil; reduce heat to low. Add flour all at once; beat with spoon until mixture forms ball. Remove from heat. Add eggs, one at a time, beating well after each addition until mixture is smooth. Drop by spoonfuls to form 12 balls on prepared cookie sheet. Bake 35 to 40 minutes or until golden brown. While puffs are warm, horizontally slice off small portion of each top; reserve tops. Remove any pieces of soft dough from inside of puffs; cool puffs on wire rack. Prepare Chocolate Cream Filling and Rich Chocolate Glaze. Fill puffs with filling; replace tops. Drizzle with prepared glaze. Garnish with fresh strawberries, if desired.

Makes 12 servings

Chocolate Cream Filling

½ cup sugar
⅓ cup all-purpose flour
½ teaspoon salt
2½ cups milk
2 egg yolks, slightly beaten
1 cup HERSHEY᾽S Semi-Sweet
   Chocolate Chips
1 tablespoon butter or margarine
2 teaspoons vanilla extract

In medium saucepan, stir together sugar, flour and salt; gradually stir in milk. Cook over medium heat, stirring constantly, until mixture comes to a boil; boil 2 minutes, stirring constantly. Gradually stir half the mixture into egg yolks; return to saucepan. Cook, stirring constantly, 1 minute. Remove from heat; stir in chocolate chips, butter and vanilla until mixture is smooth. Pour into bowl; press plastic wrap directly onto surface. Cool; refrigerate 1 to 2 hours until cold.

Rich Chocolate Glaze

½ cup HERSHEY᾽S Semi-Sweet
   Chocolate Chips
1 tablespoon shortening (do *not* use
   butter, margarine or oil)

In small microwave-safe bowl, place chocolate chips and shortening. Microwave at HIGH (100%) 1 minute; stir. If necessary, microwave at HIGH an additional 15 seconds at a time, stirring after each heating, just until chips are melted when stirred.

Cocoa Black Forest Crêpes

3 eggs
¾ cup water
½ cup light cream or half-and-half
¾ cup plus 2 tablespoons all-purpose
    flour
3 tablespoons HERSHEY'S Cocoa
2 tablespoons sugar
⅛ teaspoon salt
3 tablespoons butter or margarine,
    melted and cooled
  Cherry pie filling
  Chocolate Sauce (recipe follows)
  Sweetened whipped cream (optional)

In blender or food processor, place eggs, water and
light cream; blend 10 seconds. Add flour, cocoa, sugar,
salt and butter; blend until smooth. Let stand at room
temperature 30 minutes. Spray 6-inch crêpe pan
lightly with vegetable cooking spray; heat over medium
heat. For each crêpe, pour 2 to 3 tablespoons batter
into pan; lift and tilt pan to spread batter. Return to
heat; cook until surface begins to dry. Loosen crêpe
around edges; turn and lightly cook other side. Stack
crêpes, placing wax paper between crêpes. Keep
covered. (Refrigerate for later use, if desired.) Just
before serving, place 2 tablespoons pie filling on each
crêpe; roll up. Place crêpes, seam side down, on dessert
plate. Prepare Chocolate Sauce; spoon over crêpes.
Garnish with whipped cream, if desired.

Makes about 18 crêpes

Chocolate Sauce

¾ cup sugar
⅓ cup HERSHEY'S Cocoa
¾ cup evaporated milk
¼ cup (½ stick) butter or margarine
⅛ teaspoon salt
1 teaspoon kirsch (cherry brandy,
      optional)

In small saucepan, stir together sugar and cocoa; add
evaporated milk, butter and salt. Cook over medium
heat, stirring constantly, until mixture comes to a boil.
Remove from heat; stir in kirsch, if desired. Serve
warm. Cover; refrigerate leftover sauce.

Bananas Flambé

1 large banana
4 teaspoons honey
4 teaspoons chopped walnuts
4 teaspoons brandy (optional)

Halve unpeeled banana lengthwise; place in small
flameproof dish. Drizzle cut surface of each half with 2
teaspoons honey and sprinkle with walnuts. On top
rack of preheated oven broiler, broil banana about 5
minutes or until heated but not burnt. Remove from
broiler. If desired, pour brandy over top and flame.

Makes 2 servings

Tip: Orange blossom honey is particularly good in this
dessert.

Favorite recipe from **National Honey Board**

Individual Orange Soufflés

> 3   oranges
> 1½ tablespoons cornstarch
> 3   tablespoons orange-flavored liqueur
> 6   egg whites
> ⅛   teaspoon salt
> 6   tablespoons sugar
> 1½ tablespoons sliced almonds (optional)
> 1½ tablespoons powdered sugar (optional)

1. Preheat oven to 450°F. Spray 6 individual soufflé dishes (8 to 10 ounces each) with nonstick cooking spray. Place dishes on jelly-roll pan.

2. Grate color portion of orange peel using box-shaped grater or hand-held grater. Grate enough orange peel to equal 1½ teaspoons.

3. Cut peel and membrane from oranges; section oranges over 1-quart saucepan. Dice oranges. (There will be 1½ cups juice and pulp.)

4. Stir in cornstarch until smooth. Cook and stir over medium heat until mixture comes to a boil and thickens slightly. Remove from heat. Stir in liqueur and reserved orange peel.

5. Beat egg whites and salt with electric mixer at high speed in large bowl until soft peaks form. Gradually beat in sugar, 1 tablespoon at a time, until stiff peaks form and sugar is dissolved.

6. Fold ¼ of egg white mixture into orange mixture. Then, fold all of orange mixture into remaining egg white mixture. Spoon into prepared dishes. Sprinkle with almonds, if desired.

7. Immediately bake 12 to 15 minutes until soufflés are puffed and browned. Sprinkle with powdered sugar, if desired. Serve immediately. *Makes 6 servings*

KAHLÚA® White Chocolate Fondue

 2 **cinnamon sticks**
 ⅔ **cup whipping cream**
 6 **ounces white chocolate, chopped**
 ¼ **cup KAHLÚA®**
    Bite-size pieces of fruit, such as strawberries, raspberries, bananas, pineapple chunks, apple or orange wedges and cubes of pound cake or cookies

Cut cinnamon sticks in half lengthwise; break each half into several pieces.

Combine cream and half of cinnamon pieces in small saucepan. Bring to a rolling boil; remove from heat. Cover and let stand 15 minutes. Add remaining cinnamon pieces; return to a boil. Remove from heat. Cover and let stand 15 minutes more.

Place white chocolate in medium bowl. Return cream to a boil once more; pour through strainer into bowl with white chocolate. Discard cinnamon. Let stand 1 to 2 minutes; stir until smooth. Stir in KAHLÚA®. Serve warm in fondue pot with bite-size pieces of fruit, cake or cookies. *Makes 2 cups*

Angel Cream Dessert

20   saltine crackers
1½   cups sugar, divided
1   teaspoon baking powder
3   egg whites
⅛   teaspoon salt
1½   teaspoons vanilla extract, divided
½   cup chopped pecans
1   package (3 ounces) cream cheese, softened
1   cup miniature marshmallows
¼   cup whipping cream, whipped
½   cup sour cream
¼   cup chopped maraschino cherries
  Assorted fresh fruit (optional)

1. Preheat oven to 350°F. Grease 8-inch round baking pan. Crumble saltines by hand into coarse crumbs. Measure 1 cup; set aside.

2. Combine 1 cup sugar and baking powder in small bowl; set aside. Beat egg whites and salt in clean large bowl with electric mixer at high speed until foamy. Gradually beat in sugar mixture and 1 teaspoon vanilla until stiff peaks form.

3. Fold in cracker crumbs and pecans. Pour into prepared pan.

4. Bake 30 minutes. *Turn off oven* and let stand in oven 10 minutes. Remove from oven and cool completely (center will fall). Loosen edge and remove from pan.

5. Combine cream cheese with remaining ½ cup sugar and ½ teaspoon vanilla in large bowl. Beat with electric mixer at high speed until smooth. Gently fold in marshmallows, whipped cream, sour cream and cherries.

6. Spread over cooled base; refrigerate. Top with fresh fruit, if desired. *Makes 8 servings*

Chocolate Peanut Butter Fondue

⅓ cup unsweetened cocoa powder
⅓ cup sugar
⅓ cup 1% low-fat milk
3 tablespoons light corn syrup
2 tablespoons reduced fat peanut butter
½ teaspoon vanilla extract
2 medium bananas, cut into 1-inch pieces
16 large strawberries
2 medium apples, cored, sliced

1. Mix cocoa, sugar, milk, corn syrup and peanut butter in medium saucepan. Cook over medium heat, stirring constantly, until hot. Remove from heat; stir in vanilla.

2. Pour fondue into medium serving bowl; serve warm or at room temperature with fruit for dipping.

Makes 8 servings

HERSHEY'S White and Dark Chocolate Fudge Torte

1   cup (2 sticks) butter or margarine, melted
1½ cups sugar
1   teaspoon vanilla extract
3   eggs, separated
⅔   cup HERSHEY'S Cocoa
½   cup all-purpose flour
3   tablespoons water
1⅔ cups (10-ounce package) HERSHEY'S Premier White Chips, divided
⅛   teaspoon cream of tartar
    Satiny Glaze (recipe follows)
    White Decorator Drizzle (recipe follows)

Heat oven to 350°F. Line bottom of 9-inch springform pan with foil; grease foil and side of pan. In large bowl, combine butter, sugar and vanilla; beat well. Add egg yolks, one at a time, beating well after each addition. Blend in cocoa, flour and water. Stir in 1⅓ cups white chips. Reserve remaining chips for drizzle. In small bowl, beat egg whites with cream of tartar until stiff peaks form; fold into chocolate mixture. Pour batter into prepared pan. Bake 45 minutes or until top begins to crack slightly. (Cake will not test done in center.) Cool 1 hour. Cover; refrigerate until firm. Remove side of pan. Prepare Satiny Glaze and White Decorator

Drizzle. Pour prepared glaze over torte; spread evenly over top and side. Decorate top of torte with prepared drizzle.* Cover; refrigerate until serving time. Refrigerate leftover torte.   *Makes 10 to 12 servings*

*To decorate, drizzle with spoon or place in pastry bag with writing tip.

Satiny Glaze

1   **cup HERSHEY₅S Semi-Sweet Chocolate Chips**
¼   **cup whipping cream**

In small microwave-safe bowl, place chocolate chips and whipping cream. Microwave at HIGH (100%) 1 minute; stir. If necessary, microwave at HIGH an additional 15 seconds at a time, stirring after each heating, just until chips are melted when stirred. Cool until lukewarm and slightly thickened.

White Decorator Drizzle

⅓   **cup HERSHEY₅S Premier White Chips (reserved from torte)**
2   **teaspoons shortening (do *not* use butter, margarine or oil)**

In small microwave-safe bowl, place white chips and shortening. Microwave at HIGH (100%) 20 to 30 seconds; stir. If necessary, microwave at HIGH an additional 15 seconds at a time, stirring after each heating, just until chips are melted when stirred.

Raspberry Shortcakes

1½ cups frozen raspberries, thawed, divided
6 tablespoons sugar, divided
1 cup all-purpose flour
1 teaspoon baking powder
¼ teaspoon baking soda
1 tablespoon cold margarine
⅓ cup evaporated skim milk
1 egg white
¼ teaspoon almond extract
¾ cup 1% low-fat cottage cheese
1 teaspoon lemon juice

1. Preheat oven to 450°F. Spray cookie sheet with nonstick cooking spray. Combine 1¼ cups raspberries and 2 tablespoons plus 1½ teaspoons sugar in small bowl; cover and refrigerate until ready to serve.

2. Combine flour, 2 tablespoons sugar, baking powder and baking soda in medium bowl. Cut in margarine using 2 knives or pastry blender until mixture forms coarse crumbs; set aside.

3. In separate small bowl, beat together milk, egg white and almond extract until well blended. Add to dry ingredients; mix lightly. Place dough on lightly floured board; knead about 5 minutes or until dough is no longer sticky to the touch. Roll out dough to ½-inch thickness. Cut 8 biscuits from dough using 2½-inch biscuit cutter; place on cookie sheet. Bake 10 minutes or until tops are lightly browned. Remove to wire rack; cool.

4. Place cottage cheese, remaining 1 tablespoon plus 1½ teaspoons sugar and lemon juice in food processor; process until smooth. Transfer mixture to medium bowl. Gently stir in remaining ¼ cup raspberries.

5. Split biscuits horizontally in half; place bottom halves on individual serving plates. Top each half with about 2 tablespoons reserved raspberry mixture and 1 tablespoon cottage cheese mixture; cover with biscuit top. Top with remaining reserved raspberry and cottage cheese mixtures.   *Makes 8 servings*

White Chocolate Cheesecake

½ cup (1 stick) butter or margarine
¾ cup sugar, divided
1½ teaspoons vanilla, divided
1 cup flour
4 packages (8 ounces each) PHILADELPHIA BRAND® Cream Cheese, softened
4 eggs
2 packages (6 ounces each) BAKER'S® Premium White Chocolate Baking Squares, melted, slightly cooled

MIX butter, ¼ cup of the sugar and ½ teaspoon of the vanilla with electric mixer on medium speed until light and fluffy. Gradually add flour, mixing on low speed until blended. Press onto bottom of 9-inch springform pan; prick with fork. Bake at 325°F for 25 minutes or until edges are light golden brown.

MIX cream cheese, remaining ½ cup sugar and 1 teaspoon vanilla with electric mixer on medium speed until well blended. Add eggs, 1 at a time, mixing on low speed after each addition just until blended. Blend in melted chocolate. Pour over crust.

BAKE at 325°F for 55 minutes to 1 hour or until center is almost set. Run knife or metal spatula around rim of pan to loosen cake; cool before removing rim of pan. Refrigerate 4 hours or overnight. Garnish, if desired. *Makes 12 servings*

White Chocolate Macadamia Nut Cheesecake: Stir 1 jar (3½ ounces) macadamia nuts, chopped (about ¾ cup), into batter.

PHILLY 3-STEP™ Crème Brûlée Cheesecake

- 2 (8-ounce) packages PHILADELPHIA BRAND® Cream Cheese, softened
- ½ cup granulated sugar
- 1 teaspoon vanilla
- 2 eggs
- 1 egg yolk
- 1 ready to use graham cracker pie crust (6 ounces *or* 9 inch)
- ½ cup packed brown sugar
- 1 teaspoon water

1. MIX cream cheese, granulated sugar and vanilla at medium speed with electric mixer until well blended. Add eggs and egg yolk; mix until blended.

2. POUR into crust.

3. BAKE at 350°F, 40 minutes or until center is almost set. Cool. Refrigerate 3 hours or overnight. Just before serving, heat broiler. Mix brown sugar and water; spread over cheesecake. Place on cookie sheet. Broil 4 to 6 inches from heat 1 to 1½ minutes or until topping is bubbly. *Makes 8 servings*

Fruited Meringue Hearts Melba

6 **egg whites**
¼ **teaspoon cream of tartar**
¼ **teaspoon ground allspice**
1½ **cups sugar**
    Melba Sauce (recipe follows)
3 **cups sliced assorted fruit (berries,**
      melon, grapes)
    Mint sprigs (optional)

1. Line large cookie sheet with parchment paper; draw 6 hearts (3×3 inches) on paper.

2. Beat egg whites in large bowl with electric mixer until foamy. Add cream of tartar; beat until soft peaks form. Add allspice. Beat in sugar, 1 tablespoon at a time, beating at high speed until stiff peaks form, about 5 minutes.

3. Preheat oven to 250°F. Spoon meringue into large pastry bag fitted with medium star tip; pipe heart outlines on parchment paper. Fill in heart shapes with meringue. Then pipe second row on top of first row of meringue around outside edges of hearts to form rims.

4. Bake 1 hour or until meringues are firm and crisp to touch. Turn off oven; leave meringues in oven with door closed at least 2 hours.

5. Prepare Melba Sauce; set aside. Fill meringue hearts with fruit. Spoon about ¼ cup sauce onto each dessert plate and place filled hearts on sauce. Garnish with mint sprigs, if desired. *Makes 6 servings*

Melba Sauce

1 **package (16 ounces) frozen unsweetened raspberries, thawed, drained**
¼ **cup sugar**

Place raspberries and sugar in food processor or blender; process until smooth. Strain and discard seeds. *Makes 1½ cups sauce*

Apricot Meringue Squares

1   **cup butter, softened**
⅓   **cup granulated sugar**
1   **teaspoon vanilla extract**
2   **teaspoons grated orange peel**
2   **cups all-purpose flour**
1   **jar (12 ounces) apricot jam**
2   **tablespoons fresh orange juice**
2   **egg whites**
1   **cup powdered sugar**
    Slivered almonds (optional)

1. Preheat oven to 350°F.

2. Beat butter, granulated sugar, vanilla and orange peel in large bowl with electric mixer at medium speed until light and fluffy, scraping down side of bowl once.

3. Gradually add flour, beating at low speed until smooth.

4. Press into ungreased 13×9-inch baking pan. Bake 15 minutes. Cool completely on wire rack.

5. Combine jam and orange juice in small bowl; beat until smooth. Spread over cooled crust.

6. To make meringue, beat egg whites in clean large bowl with electric mixer at high speed until foamy. Gradually beat in powdered sugar until stiff peaks form. Spread meringue over jam with rubber spatula.

7. Bake at 350°F 15 to 20 minutes until light golden brown. Cool completely on wire rack. Cut into 2-inch squares. Garnish with almonds, if desired.

Makes about 2 dozen squares

Cherry Cake Cobbler

1 package DUNCAN HINES® Moist
   Deluxe French Vanilla Cake Mix
3 eggs
1⅓ cups water
⅓ cup CRISCO® Oil or CRISCO®
   PURITAN® Canola Oil
1 cup sugar
2 tablespoons cornstarch
2 cans (16 ounces each) pitted red tart
   cherries, undrained
2 tablespoons butter or margarine,
   melted
8 to 12 drops red food coloring
¾ teaspoon almond extract
   Whipped cream or ice cream

1. Preheat oven to 350°F. Grease and flour
13×9×2-inch pan.

2. Combine cake mix, eggs, water and oil in large
bowl. Beat at medium speed with electric mixer for
2 minutes. Pour into pan.

3. Combine sugar and cornstarch in large bowl. Add
cherries, melted butter, food coloring and almond
extract. Stir until blended. Spoon cherry mixture over
batter. Bake at 350°F for 60 to 65 minutes or until
golden. Serve warm or cold with whipped cream or ice
cream.   *Makes 12 to 16 servings*

Tip: Also delicious using DUNCAN HINES® Moist
Deluxe White Cake Mix.

Cherry Cobbler

1   cup all-purpose flour
¾   cup sugar, divided
2   tablespoons instant nonfat dry milk
      powder
2   teaspoons baking powder
¼   teaspoon baking soda
¼   teaspoon salt
2   tablespoons vegetable oil
7   tablespoons buttermilk
2   tablespoons cornstarch
½   cup water
1   package (16 ounces) frozen
      unsweetened cherries, thawed and
      drained
½   teaspoon vanilla extract
      Nonfat frozen yogurt (optional)

1. Preheat oven to 400°F. Combine flour, ¼ cup sugar, milk powder, baking powder, baking soda and salt in medium bowl. Stir in oil until mixture becomes crumbly. Add buttermilk; stir until moistened. Set aside.

2. Combine cornstarch, remaining ½ cup sugar and water in medium saucepan. Stir until cornstarch is dissolved. Cook over medium heat, stirring constantly until thickened. Add cherries and vanilla; stir until cherries are completely coated. Pour into 8-inch square baking pan; spoon biscuit mixture over cherries.

3. Bake 25 minutes or until topping is golden brown. Serve warm with nonfat frozen yogurt, if desired.

Makes 8 servings

Peach Cobbler

- 4 cups sliced peeled peaches *or* 2 (29-ounce) cans sliced peaches, drained
- 1 cup fresh or frozen blueberries (optional)
- ⅔ cup all-purpose flour, divided
- ⅓ cup sugar, divided
- 2 tablespoons lemon juice
- ⅓ cup BLUE BONNET® Vegetable Oil Spread, softened, divided
- 20 NILLA® Wafers, finely rolled (about ¾ cup crumbs)
- 2 tablespoons water

In large bowl, toss peaches and blueberries with 2 tablespoons flour, 3 tablespoons sugar and lemon juice. Place in greased 8×8×2-inch baking dish; dot with 1 tablespoon spread.

In medium bowl, combine wafer crumbs with remaining flour and sugar; cut in remaining spread until mixture resembles coarse crumbs. Stir in water until mixture holds together; shape into ball. Roll dough out between 2 sheets of lightly floured waxed paper to 7½-inch circle. Remove 1 sheet of waxed paper. Cut 1-inch circle out of center of dough. Invert dough over fruit mixture; peel off paper. Sprinkle with additional sugar if desired.

Bake at 400°F for 35 to 40 minutes or until pastry is browned. Cool slightly before serving.

Makes 8 servings

Crunch Peach Cobbler

1   can (29 ounces) or 2 cans (16 ounces
      each) cling peach slices in syrup
⅓ cup plus 1 tablespoon granulated sugar,
      divided
1   tablespoon cornstarch
½ teaspoon vanilla extract
½ cup packed brown sugar
2   cups all-purpose flour, divided
⅓ cup uncooked rolled oats
¼ cup margarine or butter, melted
½ teaspoon ground cinnamon
½ teaspoon salt
½ cup shortening
4   to 5 tablespoons cold water
      Sweetened Whipped Cream (recipe
      follows), for garnish

1. Drain peach slices; reserve ¾ cup syrup.

2. Combine ⅓ cup granulated sugar and cornstarch in small saucepan. Slowly add reserved syrup. Stir well. Add vanilla. Cook over low heat until thickened, stirring constantly. Set aside.

3. Combine brown sugar, ½ cup flour, oats, margarine and cinnamon in small bowl; stir until mixture forms coarse crumbs. Set aside.

4. Preheat oven to 350°F. Combine remaining 1½ cups flour, 1 tablespoon granulated sugar and salt in small bowl. Cut in shortening until mixture forms pea-sized pieces. Sprinkle water, 1 tablespoon at a time, over flour mixture. Toss lightly with fork until mixture holds together. Press together to form a ball.

5. Press dough between hands to form a 5- to 6-inch disk. Roll dough into square, ⅛ inch thick, on lightly floured surface. Cut into 10-inch square. Press dough onto bottom and 1 inch up sides of 8×8-inch baking dish.

6. Arrange peaches over crust. Pour sauce over peaches. Sprinkle with crumb topping. Bake 45 minutes. Prepare Sweetened Whipped Cream. Serve warm or at room temperature with Sweetened Whipped Cream.   *Makes about 6 servings*

Sweetened Whipped Cream

1 **cup whipping cream, chilled**
3 **tablespoons sugar**
½ **teaspoon vanilla extract**

Chill large bowl and beaters thoroughly. Pour chilled whipping cream into bowl and beat with electric mixer at high speed until soft peaks form. Gradually add sugar and vanilla. Beat until stiff peaks form.

Apple Cranberry Buckle

6 medium Granny Smith apples, peeled, cored, thinly sliced
¾ cup dried cranberries or dried cherries
⅓ cup orange juice
⅔ cup packed light brown sugar
1½ cups plus 2 tablespoons all-purpose flour, divided
1¼ teaspoons ground cinnamon
¼ teaspoon ground cloves
¾ cup plus 1 teaspoon granulated sugar, divided
1½ teaspoons baking powder
1 egg
⅓ cup milk
¼ cup margarine or butter, melted
1 cup apple butter
2 tablespoons amaretto liqueur (optional)

1. Preheat oven to 375°F. Place apples and cranberries in 11×7-inch baking dish. Drizzle orange juice over fruit.

2. Combine brown sugar, 2 tablespoons flour, cinnamon and cloves in small bowl. Pour over apple mixture; toss to coat.

3. Combine remaining 1½ cups flour, ¾ cup granulated sugar and baking powder in medium bowl. Add egg, milk and margarine; stir with mixing spoon to blend. Drop tablespoonfuls over top of apple mixture.

4. Sprinkle remaining 1 teaspoon granulated sugar over topping. Bake 35 minutes or until topping is lightly browned and apples are tender. Cool buckle slightly in pan on wire rack.

5. Combine apple butter and liqueur, if desired, in small microwavable bowl. Microwave at HIGH 1 minute or until warm. Spoon 1 to 2 tablespoonfuls sauce over each serving. *Makes 8 servings*

Fresh Nectarine-Pineapple Cobbler

1 DOLE® Fresh Pineapple
3 cups sliced ripe DOLE® Nectarines or Peaches
½ cup sugar
2 tablespoons all-purpose flour
½ teaspoon ground cinnamon
1 cup buttermilk baking mix
½ cup low fat or nonfat milk

• **Twist** crown from pineapple. Cut pineapple in half lengthwise. Cover and refrigerate one half for another use. Cut remaining pineapple in half lengthwise. Remove fruit from shell; core and chop fruit.

• **Combine** pineapple, nectarines, sugar, flour and cinnamon in large bowl. Spoon into 8-inch square glass baking dish.

• **Stir** baking mix and milk in small bowl until baking mix is just moistened; pour over fruit.

• **Bake** at 400°F 40 to 45 minutes or until fruit is tender and crust is lightly browned.

Makes 8 servings

The publishers would like to thank the companies and organizations listed below for the use of their recipes and photographs in this publication.

Alpine Lace Brands, Inc.
Best Foods, a Division of
 CPC International Inc.
Blue Diamond Growers
California Prune Board
California Raisin Advisory
 Board
California Strawberry
 Commission
Cherry Marketing Institute,
 Inc.
Dole Food Company, Inc.
Filippo Berio Olive Oil
Hershey Foods Corporation
Kahlúa® Liqueur
Keebler® Company

Kraft Foods, Inc.
Leaf®, Inc.
MOTT'S® Inc., a division of
 Cadbury Beverages Inc.
Nabisco, Inc.
National Honey Board
Nestlé Food Company
The Procter & Gamble
 Company
The Quaker Oatmeal
 Kitchens
Sargento® Foods Inc.
Sunkist Growers
USA Rice Council
Wisconsin Milk Marketing
 Board

VOLUME MEASUREMENTS (dry)

⅛ teaspoon = 0.5 mL

¼ teaspoon = 1 mL

½ teaspoon = 2 mL

¾ teaspoon = 4 mL

1 teaspoon = 5 mL

1 tablespoon = 15 mL

2 tablespoons = 30 mL

¼ cup = 60 mL

⅓ cup = 75 mL

½ cup = 125 mL

⅔ cup = 150 mL

¾ cup = 175 mL

1 cup = 250 mL

2 cups = 1 pint = 500 mL

3 cups = 750 mL

4 cups = 1 quart = 1 L

VOLUME MEASUREMENTS (fluid)

1 fluid ounce (2 tablespoons) = 30 mL

4 fluid ounces (½ cup) = 125 mL

8 fluid ounces (1 cup) = 250 mL

12 fluid ounces (1½ cups) = 375 mL

16 fluid ounces (2 cups) = 500 mL

WEIGHTS (mass)

½ ounce = 15 g

1 ounce = 30 g

3 ounces = 90 g

4 ounces = 120 g

8 ounces = 225 g

10 ounces = 285 g

12 ounces = 360 g

16 ounces = 1 pound = 450 g

DIMENSIONS

1/16 inch = 2 mm

⅛ inch = 3 mm

¼ inch = 6 mm

½ inch = 1.5 cm

¾ inch = 2 cm

1 inch = 2.5 cm

OVEN TEMPERATURES

250°F = 120°C

275°F = 140°C

300°F = 150°C

325°F = 160°C

350°F = 180°C

375°F = 190°C

400°F = 200°C

425°F = 220°C

450°F = 230°C

BAKING PAN SIZES

Utensil	Size in Inches/Quarts	Metric Volume	Size in Centimeters
Baking or Cake Pan (square or rectangular)	8×8×2	2 L	20×20×5
	9×9×2	2.5 L	23×23×5
	12×8×2	3 L	30×20×5
	13×9×2	3.5 L	33×23×5
Loaf Pan	8×4×3	1.5 L	20×10×7
	9×5×3	2 L	23×13×7
Round Layer Cake Pan	8×1½	1.2 L	20×4
	9×1½	1.5 L	23×4
Pie Plate	8×1¼	750 mL	20×3
	9×1¼	1 L	23×3
Baking Dish or Casserole	1 quart	1 L	—
	1½ quart	1.5 L	—
	2 quart	2 L	—